PLUM ISLAND 2017, RESURRECTION.

TABLE OF CONTENTS

Most of these chapters appeared in the Newburyport Daily News

Acknowledgements

I have mentioned most of the people who helped me gather material for this book in the text. However I would like to especially thank several people who went way beyond the call of duty.

They include Becky Coburn who designed the cover and stewarded the manuscript through the entire publication process.

They include my friend and inestimable editor at the Newburyport Daily where many of these chapters were first published.

They include the excellent photographers, Ethan Cohen and Sandy Tilton. Sandy uses her keen eye to observe the beauty of coastal processes while Ethan uses his drone to give us the big picture. Andy Griffith and Plum Island Outdoors have given us the opportunity to do much of this photography.

I would also like to thank the good people at the Quebec Labrador Foundation, The Sounds Conservancy, and the Institution for Savings, and Storm Surge for providing grants to help fund the research for this book.

And most of all I'd like to thank Kristina and Chappell for putting up with my spending long stormy nights up to my keister in cold water and long steamy days sitting on my keister typing notes in our attic.

Introduction
August 24, 2016

Ethan Cohen UVLook photo. Plum Island Point.

This is the fourth in a quartet of books that looks at Plum Island as a case study for coastal erosion. I concentrate on erosion because it neatly avoids any time wasting debates about who is causing climate change. Everyone can agree that our coasts are eroding and relate to people who are losing their homes.

My first book in this series, *Islands in the Storm,* investigated how Plum Island and other coastal communities fared before, during and after Hurricane Sandy. My second book, *Plum Island 4,000 Years on a Barrier Beach*, tried to show that this island which we like to think of as stable has actually only been around for an eye blink in geological time.

My third book, *Plum Island 2016,* concentrated on that turning point in the island's history when people started realizing that the groins, jetties and seawalls they used in the past had only increased the rate of erosion and pushed it to other parts of the island.

But in 2017 people started to work with nature, with unexpectedly good results. This is the story of that positive change.

CHAPTER I
The Drone
August 24, 2016

In August, Ethan Cohen flew his drone over Plum Island to record the condition of the beach before the arrival of the 2017 erosion season. It was a brilliant summer day and Plum Island lay out before him like a well-designed experiment.

You could see that waves struck the center of the island from the East and split to form two sand cells. One, whose longshore currents pushed sand from the center of the island north and the other, whose currents pushed sand from the center of the island south.

The island was eroding in the middle and growing at both ends. So where would you want to build a house? On the ends. And where had the houses mostly been built? In the middle.

This geological pattern had been going on for about 4,000 years. Both ends had grown several miles in the process. But that had all changed when the jetties had been built in the 1800's. They had done their job, stabilizing the mouth of the Merrimack River, but they had also blocked the sand from flowing north. Now instead of building The Point, the sand was simply collecting in a big prism behind the jetty. This was what coastal geologists called "a sink" because its sand was lost to the system of sand cells.

Without the constant influx of sand, North Point started to erode at the rate of about 150 feet a year. But that didn't last long. Waves also caused the jetty to settle, so sand could get through the jetty again. North Point started to regrow and after a few years had regrown the 400 feet worth of dunes it had lost.

The same thing happened in the Seventies when the Army Corps of Engineers repaired the jetty again. Sand was held back and North Point eroded back 400 feet. That time it was the Blizzard of 1978 that blasted several holes through the jetty and the beach, then built back the original 400 feet of sand.

You would think people would have realized what nature was trying to tell us. What we really wanted was a leaky jetty on North Point. But in 2014 the Corps repeated the same experiment with the same results. They repaired the jetty and two years later over 300 feet of well-vegetated dunes had eroded away and the 250 homes on Northern Reservation Terrace were in jeopardy. Residents had only realized it when water started flowing down well-worn paths to within 40 feet of their beachfront homes.

That crisis triggered two responses. The Massachusetts Department of Conservation and Recreation, who owned the beach, put out requests for a private firm to come up with a temporary solution to the problem and the Army Corps of Engineers started working on a long-term solution. Those two projects would be the focus of the 2017 erosion season unless nature had something else up her sleeve.

CHAPTER 2
Biomimicry
September 9, 2016

Eroded dune Plum Island point.

On September 9, the engineering firm GZA presented their short-term solution to protect the houses on Plum Island's North Point. It was an almost perfect example of mimicking nature to slow down erosion.

Another company had proposed using synthetic material and spending $500,000 to build a system that would last until the Army Corps of Engineers could find a long term solution. But the state had determined that solution was too expensive and not temporary enough.

But GZA had looked at the unique natural features of the area and then decided the best way to mimic them. There had formerly been about 400 feet of well-vegetated primary and secondary dunes protecting the neighborhood.

Such sand dunes are nature's way of protecting a barrier beach. They are perfectly designed to flex and absorb the energy of a storm. And after the storm passes, the dunes start building again. But as soon as you encase sand in a synthetic fiber, it loses its ability to shift. In effect you have created an immovable seawall, which might make people feel safer but it actually increases erosion by causing scouring around the ends of the inert sandbags.

But natural sand dunes are not just big piles of sand. Instead of being encased by an outer coating of material they are bound together internally by a matrix of dune grass rhizomes.

Dune grass is a unique plant that has evolved to live symbiotically with the dynamic environment of a constantly shifting barrier beach. A winter storm can bury dune grass under a foot of sand, and instead of dying the grass simply grows up through the sand leaving a thick latticework of spreading root-like rhizomes behind. The rhizomes then bind the sand together internally. There is nothing that humans have been able to come up with to surpass this elegant design.

So GZA decided to build two dunes, a primary dune nearest the water, and a secondary dune nearest the houses. Residents would almost certainly see waves eroding the primary dune during the coming winter, but it would not be because the dune had failed, rather because it was doing its sacrificial job.

But the first year would be the most critical one because the dune grass would not have had enough time, or storms, to grow a deep matrix of rhizomes. Plus, the so-called king tides would fall in November so that October, November and December would all have two days of ten-foot tides and about ten days of over nine foot tides. A storm was certain to occur during one of those windows of vulnerability.

But there was also a bright side to these conditions. The island would only need to have four-foot high waves to start pushing sand through the jetty. It would then collect as about an acre of sand, four feet deep on the riverside of jetty during the winter months. That would be about 5,000 cubic yards of sand, or considerably more than the amount of sand that GZA planned to add to the dunes in order to mimic the effects of winter storms.

The storms would also cause the jetty to continue to settle. It had already settled two feet by 2016. All it needed was to settle about another two feet and there would be enough sand for the beach and the dunes to start growing again. Eventually the beach would regrow the 400 feet of sand it had before the jetty was repaired.

But there was another way to keep the sand flowing. During the summer months the City of Newburyport could use a small dredge to pump sand through the jetty or a Bobcat to push it over the top. There were precedents for this in other parts of the country. The sand would then flow down along the jetty and around the spur to where bulldozers could add it to the dunes. It could also be stockpiled for future emergencies.

The city would have to get permission from the Army Corps of Engineers but this would probably not be as daunting as it sounds. After all, it was the repair of the Corps' jetty that caused the erosion in the first place.

If it did prove difficult to get permission to pump sand over the jetty, the city could always pump it directly onto the new dunes by going overland around the jetty. There, it would mimic the effects of sand blown in by the dry winds of summer.

All in all, GZA had come up with a superb design that used appropriate technology, local materials and ongoing maintenance to provide an inexpensive short-term solution so that nature could provide the long term one — for free.

CHAPTER 3
When Will This Drought Ever End?
September 19, 2016

A River Used to Run Through it. The Ipswich River.

On September 19, northern Massachusetts finally had its first decent summer rainstorm. Everyone was ecstatic. Over 90% of the state was in a severe drought. That night the weatherman announced that despite the storm the mandatory water bans would probably not be lifted.

I hated to have to write it, but these bans weren't going away any time soon. Oh sure people's lawns would start getting green again. They already had around older homes that still had American grasses naturally adapted to withstand dry conditions. It would take much longer around new houses planted with European grasses bred to be over-fertilized and watered by expensive lawn care companies.

But the bans would still be around. Most of them went into effect in June 2016. They would probably still be around in August and the bans against outside fires would not be lifted until there was snow on the ground.

The imposition of the bans had been widely divergent. Ipswich passed its ban in July when the town's rainfall fell to 10 inches below normal. Newburyport waited until September when its rainfall fell to 15 inches below normal. And even with their ban you could still see water leaking out of municipal fire hydrants and water pumping stations. And fountains spewed water into the air where it quickly evaporated over well-watered lawns. Yet when there was a fire in the Newburyport section of Plum Island Ipswich sent fire engines to help quell the flames with water from the almost empty Ipswich watershed.

This was when Ipswich only had fifteen more days of water and not enough to put out its own fires. Ipswich grass had been brown and crusty for over three months and most people were only taking one shower a week.

So when could we expect to get out of this drought? The good news was that the El Niño conditions had ended and we were entering what looked like it would be a weak La Niña system. This was when cooler waters spread across the Pacific altering the jet stream so it delivered rain, snow and frigid weather to New England particularly toward the end of the winter.

The bad news was that the so-called 2016 drought had actually started during the winter of 2015 when we had over 10 feet of snow. But the snow had been light and fluffy with very little water content. The rest of the year was relatively dry followed by a winter with almost no snow and the past summer had well below average rainfall.

So it had taken us several years to get into this drought and it would take us several years to get out of it. Plus with global warming this could represent New England's new normal, with over 90 degree days common in summer, dry autumns without colorful foliage and winters with more than our share of snow.

There had been a few silver linings to the drought. None of the shellfish beds had to be closed because of runoff, which causes high bacterial counts. Some towns even had to curtail their shellfishing season to give the beds some rest.

Plus people started to think in terms of discrete ecological units the way scientists do. Scientists study watersheds because they can measure all the water that flows into a watershed through rain gauges and all the water that flows out of a watershed through weirs in streams and rivers. Then they can measure how that water has interacted with nitrogen, carbon and mineral cycles to see how many plants, animals, trees and people the watershed can support.

Once people start thinking in terms of watersheds they start to realize we are all in this together. It matters that some towns in a watershed impose watering bans early and other towns impose them later. But it doesn't matter that someone has a private well. They were still drawing water from an aquifer fed by the common watershed. Unfortunately we will have to heed these lessons as our climate continues to deteriorate.

CHAPTER 4
The Plum Island Center for Coastal Studies;
A Modest Proposal
September 28, 2016

Stoney Stone photo. The Pink House.

On September 28, Rochelle (Rock) Joseph gaveled open the first monthly meeting of Support the Pink House. The new group had already done a magnificent job of raising awareness about saving Plum Island's iconic building. It had been built in 1922, by an embittered husband in order to spite his former wife, only to have it become a favorite subject for photographers, painters and romantics of all stripes.

The group had a year to raise money to refurbish the building or it would be demolished by the Parker River Wildlife Refuge, that was not in the business of preserving white elephants. There was general agreement that the building should be saved, but less agreement on what it should be saved for.

I decided to step into the vacuum and suggest that the Pink House could be used as a field station to study climate change and sea level rise. All you had to do was read the papers to know that humanity was facing what president Obama called the most existential threat of our lifetimes.

Nowhere was climate change more apparent than on barrier beaches, and for years Plum Island had provided the perfect example of everything that you shouldn't do on a barrier beach. More recently, however Plum Island had started to become a showplace for how humans could work with nature to adapt to the effects of sea level rise. At the same time they also had to work to reduce climate change.

If there was a field station on Plum Island, it would be close to Boston's many schools and colleges studying these problems.

During the past year alone, over a hundred students from North Andover worked with the University of New Hampshire to plant four large plots of dune grass on Plum Island's North Point. And almost a hundred additional students from North Shore high schools mapped and profiled Plum Island's beaches with funding from a federal sustainability grant given out in the wake of Hurricane Sandy.

And scores of graduate students from places like the Virginia Institute of Marine Sciences, Boston University, the Woods Hole Group and the Army Corps of Engineers had lived on the island while conducting research. Plus senior scientists from across the country studied the Plum Island Estuary at the Marine Biological Laboratory's Marsh House facility in Rowley, along with throngs of undergraduates from Boston area colleges that took field trips to the island to study its fauna and flora.

Despite all these activities, there was no central station where groups could have access to boats, equipment and laboratories to record their findings and present them to the public.

The Plum Island Center for Coastal Studies could be that facility. Its researchers would introduce students to the island and provide vans to take them to Center Groin, Sandy Point and North Point where they could participate in ongoing projects to chronicle the erosion and growth of the island.

The Center could also provide research boats and kayaks so students could dive for specimens in the Plum Island estuary and potentially connect with scientists from the MBL's Marsh House lab, studying the water and nitrogen cycles of the estuary and its adjacent watersheds. Plus, students could help band endangered species of birds with researchers from Joppa Flats and the Wildlife Refuge.

The Center would provide these services to groups on day long or weekend field trips as well as to students conducting long term research while living on the island or in Newburyport. The visiting institutions could either pay for these services individually or rent a lab bench and equipment for an entire year.

In the end, the Center could be a catalyst for linking the resources already offered at the Refuge, Mass Audubon, the MBL, the MRBA, PITA, the Plum Island Foundation Storm Surge and Support the Pink House.

CHAPTER 5
Droning On
October 18, 2016

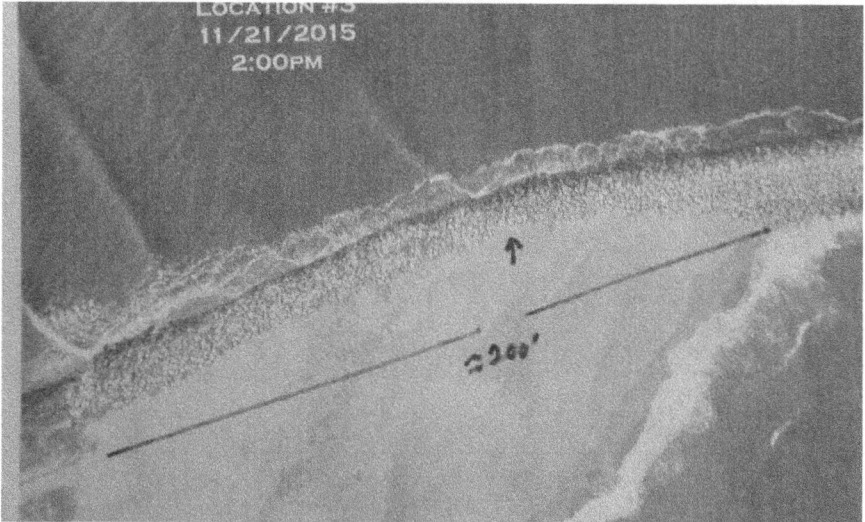

LOCATION #3
11/21/2015
2:00PM

~200'

Ethan Cohen UAVLook. Drone shot of South Jetty.

In mid-October, Ethan Cohen and I trekked out to the end of the Merrimack River's South Jetty. For the past year we had been using Ethan's drone to take aerial photos of the jetty every three months at low tide for a small contract we had with the Newburyport Conservation Commission.

The photos had already shown that about an acre of sand four feet deep flowed through the jetty during the winter months. Then it took about three weeks for each acre of sand to snake its way down along the jetty, and come to rest on North Point Beach. So we knew that about 30,000 cubic yards of sand was being removed from behind the jetty every winter. But we were about to find out something even more astonishing.

When the drone reached 400 feet, Ethan shouted back to me, "Come over and take a look at this. When we took this same shot last October you could see the whole prism of sand in the frame. Now it doesn't fit."

I squinted into the monitor and sure enough, the longshore currents had added a pie shaped wedge of sand about 50 feet wide and almost a quarter of a mile long and we hadn't even noticed it! This meant that about 50,000 cubic yards of sand were now in position to flow through the jetty when the jetty settled two more feet, and maybe 100,000 cubic yards if the jetty settled another four feet.

But this would be OK because the beach would be close to a state of equilibrium, in which about the same amount of sand flowing through the jetty would be being replaced above the jetty. And this would be enough for North Point Beach to start growing again.

When we projected the photographs for the Conservation Commission members, we showed them that you could also zoom in to see where several 4 foot deep gullies had already formed in the jetty... to say nothing of a close-up of "Roxy the jetty dog," who I had come to know in my weekly inspections of the jetty during the summer.

The photos allowed us to get our feet wet with this powerful new technology, but we also realized that we had just skimmed the surface of what could be done. If we rented special software we could program the drone so it would automatically fly a grid over the jetty, taking several shots from slightly different angles.

The software would then stitch the photos together into a 3-D profile that would be accurate to the nearest half-inch which should be powerful enough to see the jetty disheveling. The software could also tell us the exact volume of sand in a particular sand dune. This feature could be crucial in both designing and maintaining the twin dune system that the state planned to start building by the end of the month.

More crucially, the software could allow Newburyport to tell FEMA exactly how much the dunes had eroded during a particular declared emergency. This might then put FEMA on the hook for replacing the state funded dunes as part of the island's "infrastructure," a pretty big bang for the city's buck.

CHAPTER 6
King Tide Mischief
Crane's Beach
October 16, 2016

King tide, Crane's Castle.

On October 16 Randy Hackett asked his daughter's boyfriend, Alex, whether he wanted to join Randy on his regular evening swim. The two donned thick neoprene wetsuits and entered the water on Crane's Beach at 5:15 pm.

Randy and Alex figured they would have just enough time to swim several miles before the beach closed at 5:50. The water was still 60 degrees, unseasonably warm for this time of year, and there were no waves — almost perfect weather for the 58-year old triathlon athlete and his 28-year-old companion.

But after only ten minutes of swimming parallel to the shore, the two were enveloped in a thick blanket of fog. Randy couldn't see his own hands, let alone see Alex swimming beside him.

Randy yelled to Alex that they should head back to the beach. But it was too late. They were caught in rip current made unusually strong by the unique celestial conditions overhead. Although they couldn't see the moon, it was full and almost 30,000 miles closer to the earth than usual.

Plus, the earth was as close to the sun as it would be for almost 30 years. This was the perfect recipe for what have become know as "king tides", high tides that pass through the tide chart like pigs in a python. Simple king tides occur every 14.5 months, stronger king tides every 14.5 years and the strongest king tides every 30 years, and it was these that had helped create the stronger, more capricious currents they were experiencing.

All that Randy and Alex knew was that you shouldn't try to fight a rip current, but to swim parallel to the shore until you found still water. But that was easier said than done in the fog and rapidly gathering darkness.

Randy heard Alex's voice grow fainter and fainter and then he was alone, unsure which way to swim. He checked his watch. It was 6:30 and the beach should be closed. He hoped his wife had called the police.

He figured he had already drifted several miles down the beach, so he decided to conserve energy. He started relying on his wetsuit to keep him afloat while he switched from swimming breaststroke and sidestroke, then floating on his back to prevent cramping.

"Relax Randy," he told himself, trying not to think about the Great White sharks that were still in these waters at this time of year. He knew the gelatinous bodies brushing against his face were only innocuous ctenophores not stinging jellyfish, but still. "Don't panic Randy boy. With luck you should be able to make it to daylight."

But after spending the same two hours in the water, Alex had been able to swim ashore and walk back to the command post set up by rescue personnel at the behest of Randy's wife. Between gulps of warm tea to fight off hypothermia, Alex was able to tell the officers that Randy was probably several miles down the beach and almost a quarter of a mile offshore.

Around 8:15pm the fog lifted and Randy was able to see the moon for the first time all evening, but it was enough to allow him to get his bearings and start swimming purposefully toward shore. After about an hour, a glow of lights appeared on the horizon and Randy realized he had not been alone all these hours, his friends and family had been trying to save him.

Five minutes later Randy heard the chop of a Coast Guard helicopter flying a quarter mile grid along the shore. It grew closer and closer until he was bathed in the beam of their welcoming searchlight. He had never been so happy to see anyone as the diver they lowered into the water to strap Randy into the lift harness.

As they were being lifted into the warm glowing maw of the helicopter the diver yelled into Randy's ear, "Hey man I like your wetsuit. It's the same model as mine."

Randy didn't know if rescuers were trained to make small talk under such emotional conditions, but he had also never been so happy to hear small talk in all his life.

But that was not the full extent of the king tides' mischief. The day before, rapid currents flowing out of the Merrimack River had flipped a 53-foot tuna boat throwing two men into the water who had to be saved by a nearby boat.

And waves and currents had torn 21 feet off the dunes on Plum Island's North Beach. The same thing had happened during last year's king tides when the wing bar had focused erosion on the north end of the beach in September then shifted to focus it on the south end of the beach during the winter. Plum Island was back to having close to the most erosion of any beach on the East Coast and the highest of all the year's king tides would return in November.

CHAPTER 7
The Mystery of the Fossilized Oyster; Crane's Beach
October 23, 2016

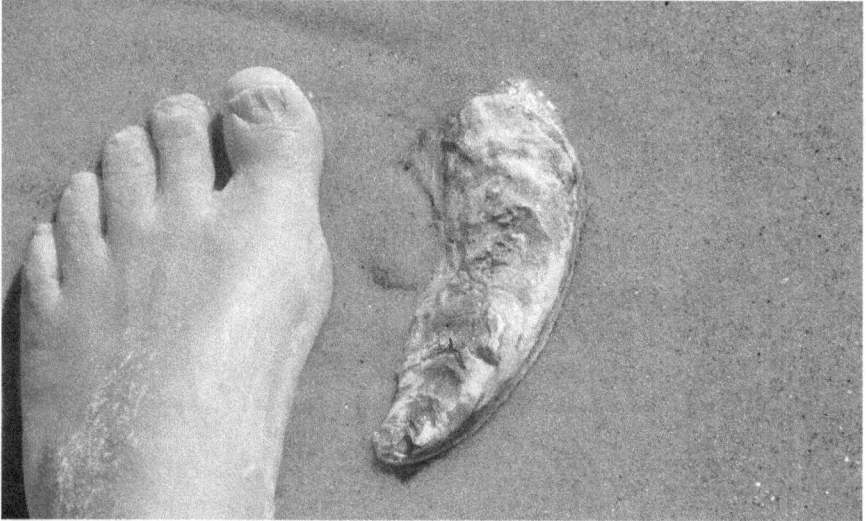

Fossilized oyster

On October 23, I decided to take advantage of some of the king tides' extreme low tides to dig some surf calms. The end of Plum Island had grown so far south that it had displaced the Parker River. So the river's currents were now cutting into the end of Crane's Beach, in Ipswich.

Ever since last February these currents had kicked surf clams out of the sand, stranding so many of the 5-inch long bivalves in windrows that the Ipswich shellfish warden declared that no permit would be needed to collect the clams before they died.

The week before, stormy weather had also kicked thousands of immature surf clams out of the sand where they had sat in large piles, thrashing their feet in and out vainly trying to dig back into the sand before being eaten by seagulls. They reminded me of inch-long coquina clams that you see in Florida.

So I expected to see large numbers of dead surf clams. But I didn't expect to see hundreds of northern quahog shells interspersed with oyster shells. And they were not like modern oyster shells, they were long and thin and had the patina of old age.

But oysters live in protected waters. How did they get on an ocean-facing beach? There were no beds of modern oysters near enough to account for such high concentrations, and the shells were too dispersed to be from middens. Besides the shells looked like they were thousands of years old not hundreds of years old, so what was going on here thousands of years ago?

We know that Plum Island formed about half a mile offshore and had been pushed to its present location by the rising seas. But about 2,000 years ago the island ran into drumlins that had anchored it in place. Since then, the beach has been remarkably stable except for the waves that continue to erode the center of the island and cause its ends to grow.

That growth has gradually pushed the mouth of the Parker River south. But 2,000 years ago it was still about half a mile north of its present location as was a headland of sand and glacial till that extended north from the Ipswich side of the river. The Crane estate sits on this drumlin today.

But 2,000 years ago the headland stretched about a quarter of a mile north along with the spit of sand, which stretched south off the headland. Today we call that spit of sand Crane's Beach. But Crane's Beach was also about a quarter of a mile east of its present location and it probably protected a marsh and estuary with extensive oyster beds along its backside.

During the intervening years, Crane's Beach had gradually rolled over these areas burying the ancient oyster beds and it is only today that the king tide and rising seas are unearthing their fossilized shells.

When I returned home I e-mailed Chris Hein whose graduate students from the Virginia Institute of Marine Science had been studying the south end of Plum Island for the past few years. He corroborated my theory and urged me to collect a few of the oyster shells so they could be carbon dated to determine their age.

That was fine with me. It would necessitate another expedition to Crane's Beach. Not bad for a day's work.

CHAPTER 8
Reflections on Erosion
Plum Island Point
October 29, 2016

Plum Island Point erosion.

On October 29, I joined some citizen scientists measuring erosion on Plum Island Point. It was high tide and large waves were breaking over the jetties and running far up on the shore. I hadn't been on the beach for close to a month and at first it was hard to get my bearings.

During the summer, I had led groups out here every week at both the high and low tides. So I had known about what to expect. A beach is different every day, but if you visit it often enough you get a feel for what is happening. But we had just entered the stormy Northeaster season so the waves were high and getting even higher as they rode on top of the ten-foot king tides.

The combined forces had eroded 31 feet off the dunes on the north end of the beach, and 6 feet off the dunes in the center of the beach. This tracked closely with what happened the year before when the erosion had started on the north end of the beach, then moved south during the winter months. We felt this was influenced by the seasonal shifting of a so-called wing bar of sand that focused erosion on different parts of the beach.

One of the photographers had taken a shot of four-foot deep sinkholes beside the jetty, so I was also eager to get out there before high tide. But we were disappointed; sand was only flowing through the jetty near the ocean. I hadn't realized that the photograph of the sinkholes had been from the landward end of the jetty where sand had blown in from an adjacent dune. This was something we hadn't seen so dramatically in 2016.

But the far end of the jetty didn't totally disappoint. In addition to a few waves breaking over the top of the jetty from the oceanside, other waves were washing under the jetty from the riverside. We could see water from the waves rushing through the boulders four feet below us.

We could also see the results. The waves had washed rocks and sand from under the large boulders, causing them to settle and crack. In the beginning of the summer you could just fit your hand in some of the cracks in the boulders, now they were three inches wide.

So the beach erosion had started in earnest, as had the settling of the South Jetty. Now we were in a race to see which would happen first; waves reaching the houses on Northern Reservation Terrace, or waves settling the jetty enough so the beach could start growing again.

If it was a calm year the erosion would probably win, but if it was a stormy year settling could be the victor. This is what had happened so dramatically during the Blizzard of 1978.

Several of our citizen scientists had posted photographs of the rapid erosion brought on by the month's storms and king tides. Some were ephemeral and quite beautiful like the one of a dune whose eroding face looked like a row of symmetrical hamlets clinging to the edge of limestone pinnacles in inland China.

On the way home we discussed how we felt about such erosion. It was certainly frightening if it was advancing toward your home and it was certainly sad if you felt it was destroying what had been your favorite childhood beach.

But I had to admit I also found it fascinating. There are very few places on our planet where you could witness such rapid geological change. The southern end of Plum Island grows almost a quarter of a mile longer every year. An astronomer sitting on Mars could see it growing. The northern end of Plum Island wants to grow just as fast but it is locked up in half a million cubic yard prism of sand behind the newly repaired jetty.

We had seen the beach above the jetty grow as much as 100 feet toward the ocean as long period waves had welded offshore sandbars onto the beach during a single tidal cycle. It was more difficult to see such growth than to see waves eroding away great chunks of dunes. Growth was more subtle but in ways infinitely more awe-inspiring.

It was equally fascinating to realize that we had just witnessed one split second in the earth's timeless cycle of geology. One day it would mold this sand into sedimentary sandstone, heat it into quartzite then raise it into a towering new mountain range of schist that would be already eroding sand back toward a new beach — half a billion years in the future.

CHAPTER 9
The MRBA
November 4, 2016

MRBA members.

On November 4, I attended the monthly meeting of the Merrimack River Beach Users Alliance. The MRBA is a unique coalition of local, state and federal officials that prides itself on always having all the disparate players sitting around the same table.

But today there was a palpable sense of fear and expectation in the room, expectation that the upcoming erosion season was going to be particularly long and dangerous; and fear that nobody was really prepared to deal with it.

Residents on Northern Reservation Terrace had watched October's king tides wash thirty feet of sand off the dunes in front of their houses during the particularly stormy month. What would happen when the king tides returned in November, when the moon would be 30,000 miles closer to the earth than any time in the past 70 years?

In the old days people figured that the erosion season ran from December through March. In fact the National Lifesaving Service only paid surfmen to patrol the beaches during those four months. But in recent years the king tides have extended the erosion season. In 2015, erosion had started when the king tides had peaked in September. This year the erosion season would really get cooking when the king tides peaked in November. In 2018 they would peak on January 2.

There was fear in the room, because everyone knew that they really weren't prepared. The engineers at GZA were frustrated because the state had been dragging their feet about giving them permits to start creating the twin dune system in front of Northern Reservation Terrace. It was ironic that a project designed to protect dunes had been held up while bureaucrats checked to make sure no needle grass would be disturbed.

The delays meant that GZA would not be able to start planting dune grass until December when it wouldn't have time to grow a matrix of rhizomes to hold the dunes together. So the artificial dunes would be no more than two piles of loose sand during the critical first year of the project.

Nothing had really happened about a plan to stockpile sand in case erosion broke through the island. Mayor Holladay noted rather pointedly that the sand Newburyport had put in Newbury's Olga's Way for both communities to use in the case of an emergency had disappeared at least four times. Many suspected the sand had ended up in front of private homes in Newbury.

As the meeting proceeded it became clear that despite past discussions about sand bags and long term solutions, all the communities planned to do, and about all they could do in the event of a severe erosion emergency, was to shut off the water and sewer mains and evacuate the island.

CHAPTER 10
The Donald Goes to the Beach;
What Can We Do?
November 9, 2016

New beach houses going up in New Jersey.

On November 9, the unthinkable happened. Donald Trump won the Presidency. It was like climate change; everyone knew he was coming, nobody did anything about it, and now it was too late.

But the election got me thinking. There is a strictly conservative way to deal with erosion and a strictly liberal way to deal with erosion.

The liberal way is to basically do what we are doing now, provide federal flood insurance to homeowners and federal assistance to rebuild the infrastructure after a storm passes. The strictly conservative way to deal with erosion would be to have private companies insure homeowners and let markets solve the problem. This is what was happening until the Nineties when private insurance companies started getting out of the business because storms had increased and it was getting too risky.

Just to make matters even more confusing, there is also a strict constructionist way to deal with erosion; if a state passes a regulation that lowers the value of someone's home, the state is required to reimburse the owner under a strict reading of the takings clause of the 5th amendment to the Constitution.

But now the reason that the problem is so confusing is that so many wealthy people live on the shore. Even though they might not want the government to give money to other people, they are more than happy to take government money for themselves.

The problem with the 5th amendment is that it was written for land that doesn't move. It provided much needed protection against the police powers of the state under those circumstances. It was only when the Supreme Court extended the amendment to coastal areas that it became problematic.

During the Seventies, states had passed regulations that discouraged people from building on places like barrier beaches because scientists had discovered that such beaches had to be able to move in response to the rising seas. But developers started challenging the laws. By 1992, Lucas vs. South Carolina Coastal Council had worked its way up to the Supreme Court where the justices ruled that if a state passed a law that lowered the value of someone's property the state would have to compensate the owner.

This takings ruling threw a monkey wrench into states' abilities to protect both the coasts, and homeowners from building on beaches that were destined to wash away. It was a festering problem when the seas were only rising a foot every century. But now we know the seas may rise three feet higher in twenty-five years and nine feet higher in fifty years, so it has become an acute problem. This amount of sea level rise will put millions of homes worth billions of dollars in jeopardy, and states will be unable to save people from risking their life savings on such dubious investments.

If Hilary Clinton had been elected President she might have been able to put enough liberal Supreme Court justices on the Court to overturn Lucas vs. South Carolina. Now it may take eight years, or a few more storms in quick succession, to see if President Trump can adapt the safeguards of our liberal democracy to deal with the realities of our rapidly changing environment. You won't see me holding my breath.

So if it was clear that nothing substantial would be done about climate change for at least the next four years, what should individuals and small groups do to deal with the effects of that global warming?

For one thing, we had our own barrier beach that protects the communities of Newbury, Newburyport, Rowley and Ipswich. We had started to make progress in educating people to think like coastal geologists. A coastal geologist would look at Plum Island and say that you should discourage people from rebuilding homes in the center of the island, but help the island continue to grow on its north and south ends.

That educational process had started and new groups like Storm Surge and the Plum Island Point Preservation organization could continue to work with older groups like the MRBA, PITA and the Plum Island Foundation to search for better, more local, ways to deal with erosion on our own all important barrier beach island.

Education has always been the Massachusetts way. Who knew in four years the Feds would look at Massachusetts as a model for how to deal with the effects of erosion and sea level rise?

CHAPTER 11
The Super Moon
November 13, 2016

Super moon.

On a whim I decided to go to North Point to photograph the moon, which had not been this close to the earth since 1948. Because these super moons have a 14.5-year cycle, I had only seen 4 of them in my lifetime.

All of them were memorable. One helped create the "New Inlet" in Chatham. Another occurred when I was studying monkeys on an island off Puerto Rico.

A small group of us had been living on the beach with its constant roar of the surf, so one night I decided to climb through a deep ravine to spend a night with the monkeys. I finally found the monkeys quietly sitting on an exposed ridge, grooming each other while gazing toward the East. This seemed odd because tropic birds were staging aerial duels against a Wagnerian sunset to the west.

But suddenly a huge moon rose rapidly over the distant villages of Puerto Rico. I felt like I was on another planet. The moon was so preternaturally large and rising that quickly because we were so close to the equator.

The monkeys seemed equally enraptured. I had the distinct feeling that they had gathered on this exposed promontory to see the moon rise, which meant they knew how to tell time, which was so intimately connected with ancient human religions.

But having a sense of time didn't really seem so strange under these circumstances. We had been sleeping under the stars all summer and when we woke up at night it had become almost second nature to tell what time it was by seeing which constellation had just risen or set above us. It did not seem so far-fetched that the monkeys had a similar sense of nature's time.

CHAPTER 12
The Dual Dune System
November 16, 2016

Darryl Forgione.

I went back to Plum Island on November 16 to photograph the king tide that usually lags behind the super moon by a few days. It was damp, dark and depressing, gravid with the potential for rain.

When I entered the North Point parking lot, fresh water was gurgling up through the asphalt. The king tide had pushed the water table so high that the lens of fresh water that floats on the salt water under the island had been pushed to the surface and was pooling up along the edge of the lot.

Environmentalists call this "nuisance flooding" and warn that it will become more and more prevalent as the seas rise. What they forget is that this was the highest tide of the year and the king tides would be steadily declining for the next 7 years.

This would play right into the hands of Donald Trump's climate denying appointees to the EPA and the Department of the Interior. The king tide's yearly reminders of the effects of sea level rise would become less and less severe during Trump's potential two terms. Then, when the king tides peak again in 15 years, the damage will have been done and the king tides will be riding on top of an additional three feet of sea level rise. And barrier beaches like Plum Island will be a breaking up and washing away.

The second thing I noticed was a big pile of sand at the far end of the lot. Three trucks had been delivering sand from a quarry in Maine all morning. The idea was to use this slightly darker sand to build a dune close to the water and use sand George Charos had dredged from underneath his dock on the end of North Point to build up a dune in front of the houses on Northern Reservation Terrace. It would take about a week to construct each dune and ten days to plant dune grass to bind the dunes together.

By the time I reached the end of the South Jetty the high tide had already peaked, but I could see where waves had pushed sand through the boulders the night before. When we first noticed that the jetty had settled, it was on a stretch of the jetty that was only about twenty feet long. That was less than a year ago. Now the stretch where the jetty had settled had grown to 125 feet and the base of the jetty was so wide that it was much easier for fishermen to climb down to the water's edge. It also looked like that area of the jetty had settled a few more inches since June.

On my way back I bumped into Darryl Forgione who was overseeing the dual dune system for the state Department of Conservation and Recreation. He was pleased, all the permits had finally been granted and the project was underway.

So now we were in a race to see which would happen first. Would storms break through the two dunes and reach the houses on Northern Reservation Terrace or would the jetty settle enough so the beach would start growing again? I doubt that even Jimmy the Greek would dare to give you odds on either outcome. It would all depend on weather and the weather is a rogue.

CHAPTER 13
Our Settling Jetty
November 18, 2016

Dip where the jetty has settled.

On November 18, our group of citizen scientists compared our photographs taken before and after the peak of the king tides. We all felt that the jetty had settled during the last two months but didn't have a way to quantify the change, so we decided to go back through our old photographs.

I remembered I had a few shots that I took when the Corps first started repairing the jetty. They showed that the jetty had been designed with a flat top so trucks and excavators could drive out on the jetty as they built it seaward. Plus the armored sides of the jetty were smooth with evenly placed boulders so they could deflect the blows of the incoming waves.

But I was also able to find some photos taken after a second contractor had been hired to finish the job. Gone were the smoothly armored sides. It looked like rocks had just been dumped haphazardly down the sides of the jetty in order to finish before April 1. That was the deadline when all heavy equipment had to be off the beach so the endangered piping plovers could start laying their eggs.

When the jetty started settling, you sometimes had eight to ten-foot high waves pounding it from both sides. The waves would swirl under and around the lower rocks causing them to settle, which would make the rocks above them slump as well.

Joe Teixeira from the Newburyport Conservation Commission pointed out that each wave would also make the entire jetty vibrate causing the boulders to shift a tiny fraction of an inch; every second of every minute, every minute of every hour and every hour of every year. This assault was the same as what was happening to Newbury's seawalls that had failed every year because of the continual onslaught.

But it was even more complicated than that. When we first noticed that the jetty was settling, it was only along a 25-foot stretch of boulders where the waves were pounding the jetty from both sides.

But the waves had also built up the beach seaward. This had blocked the surf from undermining the jetty from the oceanside, but they had kept on pounding it from the riverside.

So the stretch of jetty being undermined had been greatest where the waves had been undermining it from the both sides. But this area had also expanded, as the beach had grown seaward. Now, that original area had grown from just 30 feet long to 125 feet long in less than a year.

The question was, would the sand flow through that entire length of the jetty during upcoming storms? We would have to see as the erosion season progressed.

CHAPTER 14
The Sound of a Bubble Bursting
November 24, 2016

The sound of a Bubble Bursting?

On November 24, the New York Times ran a cover story that quoted South Florida Mayor Phillip Stoddard as saying, "Coastal mortgages are growing into as big a bubble as the housing market of 2007. But this time there will be no rebound because the water wont recede and properties will eventually lose their value."

And I thought it would be a major storm that would wake everyone up, not the sound of a bubble bursting. Silly me, I forgot that most people don't think of storms all the bloody time. They use what Alan Greenspan called "irrational exuberance" to make economic decisions.

The article included graphics that showed how county- by-county housing sales had declined by 4 percent in the last five years on the East Coast, while sales of inland homes had risen seven percent. The writer quoted a Miami Beach resident who planned to move inland in anticipation of higher king tides and wrote that people's concerns had taken on a new urgency since the election of Donald Trump. In 2012 Trump had famously said, "Global warming is just a concept created by the Chinese in order to make U.S. manufacturing non-competitive."

Frankly I think the writer was wrong to politicize his argument and conflate king tides with sea level rise, because we know that king tides will actually be declining during the four or eight years that Trump will be in office.

But his economic analysis was spot on. Potential home buyers are becoming leery of being tied into paying thousands of dollars for federal flood insurance and tens of thousands of dollars to rebuild collapsed seawalls and raise their homes on pilings.

But will the coastal housing bubble burst or deflate like the Patriots' footballs during the Superbowl? Plum Island supports the deflationary model.

After a March storm destroyed eight houses and made twenty uninhabitable on Plum Island in 2013, the cost of the lots plummeted. But two years later the price of the empty lots had risen back to about what they had been before the storm.

A few sharp developers and home buyers bought the lots right after the storm when their prices were still rock bottom. Then a game of hot potato began.

Developers rushed to build homes and sell them before the next major storm. Banks earned commissions on these risky mortgages then sold them as bundled securities to unsuspecting pension funds, insurers or other buyers. The point of the game was not to be left holding the bag.

Efforts to ensure that real estate agents disclose the erosional history of oceanfront homes have run into stiff opposition. One law in Virginia ended up explicitly stating that the seller of a house was not obligated to disclose whether the house was in a high risk FEMA zone. The head of the Virginia Association of Realtors said they were "immensely satisfied" with the law—no doubt!

Measures to require that investors be told what portion of their bundled mortgages included houses in areas at risk from storms, canyon fires, earthquakes, tsunamis and tornadoes have fared equally well.

Most interestingly, Robert Meyer, the co-director of the Risk Management and Design Processes Center at the Wharton Business School has found that people living in places like Miami would be willing to pay billions of dollars in extra taxes in order to pay for infrastructure so they could continue living on that unpredictable coast.

But that is another economic analysis also based on irrational exuberance. A geological analysis would say that there are no infrastructural changes that will allow people to continue living on barrier beaches for the next 30 to 50 years.

CHAPTER 15
The Big Tuna
November 29, 2016

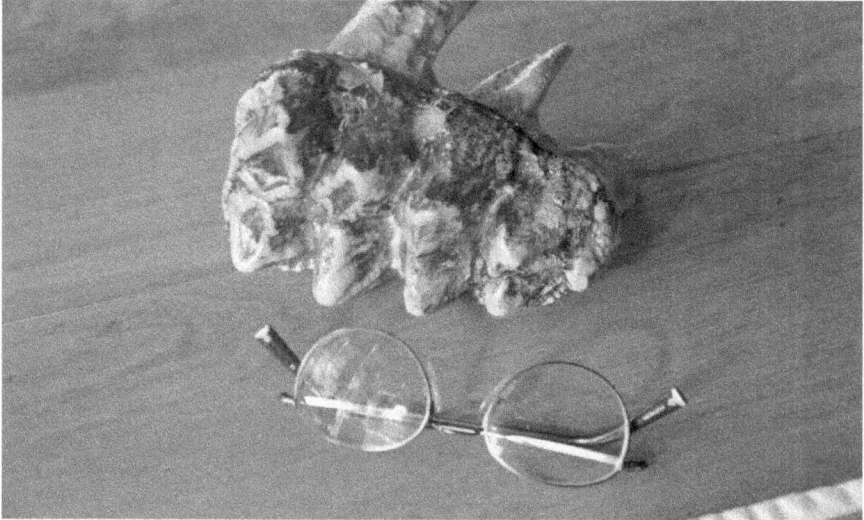

Baby Mastodon tooth brought up in a net off Plum Island by Peter Atherton.

Back in October, I had read a piece in the Newburyport Daily News about a tuna boat capsizing in the dangerously shallow waters off the mouth of the Merrimack River. It got me thinking, why hadn't I read more about this colorful local fishery?

I knew that tuna fishermen were the rock stars of other ports. In Chatham tourists would line up every evening to see the tuna boats come in and the fishermen wouldn't disappoint.

The harpooners had long flowing hair, well muscled torsos and were always topless, as they used long thin knives to cut and clean their fish. A quick intake of breath would ripple through the female members of the audience when the fishermen turned the hoses on each other to wash off the blood and gore. They were New England's matadors.

Massachusetts lands more Bluefin Tuna than any other state and Newburyport has always been one of fishery's busiest ports, but why I had never read any stories or seen any photographs of this important local fishery? Was it because the Feds had shut the fishery down, that Newburyport was more interested in urban concerns, or was it something else?

Through a circuitous route that involved a chance encounter at a doctor's office and the generous gift of Doug Whynott's excellent book, *Giant Bluefin*, I discovered that one of the best tuna fishermen was semi-retired and living on Plum Island. Peter Atherton had just become a grandfather for the third time the day before I called. He was 68 years old.

Peter remembered "the good old days" in 1989 when a profusion of sand eels had brought both the tuna and whales within six miles of the shore. "It was like 9 to 5 that year. In the mornings you would be harpooning giant tuna right beside bulky Humpback whales surging up through circles of bubbles they had blown to encircle huge schools of the baitfish. Then at about four in the afternoon you would move offshore to see 'the show' when almost the entire population of the medium sized Bluefin came to the surface to feed. Sometimes you would see 1,200 of the six-foot long iridescent fish charging through the water."

In the Nineties, spotter pilots and scientists from the New England Aquarium used photographs of these "shows" to prove that the mathematical models used by the National Marine Fisheries Service had underestimated the population of Bluefin Tuna in the Western Atlantic.

That year you would often see eight or nine boats lined up at Newburyport's Tri-Coastal docks to unload the fish and truck them to Logan airport. From there they could be flown to Tokyo to be auctioned at the Tsukiji fish market the next morning. Nobody knew it then, but 1989 would be close to the peak of the fishery in terms of catch, if not profits.

In the Nineties, Royko Mirawaka, the head of the Toschi seafood trading company spent the summer in Newburyport teaching the fishermen of the Tri-Coastal cooperative how to preserve their fish in order to get top dollar. The fish would be graded four times; at the dock, before shipping, on arrival and at auction in Tokyo.

The instructions and relationships the fishermen and buyers forged worked to everyone's benefit. Fishermen were able to sell the well marbled tuna caught at the end of the season for as much as $44,000 a fish, enough for a down payment on a house; and Japanese restaurants were able to sell deep red Maguro tuna for $77 a mouthful. They served the Maguro on white plates to enhance the tuna's color because Japanese people eat with their eyes before they eat with their stomachs.

Peter also remembered when a dozen fishermen flew down to Washington in their spotters' planes to show the delegates of the International Tuna Commission their photos of the afternoon "shows". Although the photos proved that the science was wrong, the quotas kept coming down as more and more boats entered the fishery.

But it was never an even game. Of the thousand of boats pursuing the tuna only about 700 would catch a single fish and only about a hundred would catch more than one fish. In the old days about twelve boats would fill the harpoon quota. Now about 30 boats were filling the quota but making a lot less money while doing it.

Peter also remembered listening to the rescue attempts of his friend Jeff Hutchins captain of the *Heather Lynne II* who also part of the Tri-Coastal fishermen's cooperative. Another friend, Kevin Smith had been lying at anchor in the early morning when he heard a tugboat frantically blowing its horn, then there was a huge whack as the barge the tugboat was towing hit the *Heather Lynne*.

Kevin steamed to the spot and leaned over to tap the hull of the overturned boat with his harpoon. Thank God someone was alright. He was tapping back through the hull and the Coast Guard was on their way. That was at about 4:00 am. But when the Coast Guard arrived about half an hour later, the *Heather Lynne* started to right herself. There was a big whoosh of air then silence. Whoever had been tapping back had just drowned. The divers that the Coast Guard requested from another agency had never arrived.

It had been a difficult lesson for someone like Peter who had served in Vietnam. Any sense of security that the Coast Guard would do anything possible to save you had slipped away along with the lives of the three fishermen lost on that unforgettable day.

CHAPTER 16
An Unsettling Beach Walk
December 1, 2016

Dog watches as man retrieves his ball in 4 foot waves.

December 1 was a warm, sunny, late autumn day. I hadn't bothered to check on the tides because I only intended to take pictures of the two new artificial dunes, so I was pleasantly surprised when I realized I had arrived at the high tide and long period waves were crashing against the shore.

As I approached the south jetty, I photographed a man dashing down to the water's edge to retrieve his dog's ball. My next photo saw the man tripping as he tried to race back up the berm before the next eight-foot high wave engulfed him. Fortunately the next wave wasn't quite strong enough to pull him back into the maelstrom. I told him I would have felt awful if I was sitting there taking pictures as he was swept out to sea. We laughed, but it had been a little too close for comfort.

Then we turned our attention to the tide. Something was strange about it. We were only supposed to have a seven-foot tide, but this one was over ten feet high. The waves were long period waves from yesterday's distant storm and they were working in tandem to hold the high tide up against the shore. One wave would push about two feet of water up against the beach then the next wave would ride on top of the first delivering even more water. So, wave-by-wave they had managed to raise the tide three feet higher than usual and hold it there for almost an hour longer than usual.

But something else was also going on. You could see a sandbar underneath the surface. The waves were washing sand off the bar and using it to build up a ten-foot high ridge of sand along the shore. What we were actually seeing was the offshore sandbar welding onto the beach. The ridge was so high that waves couldn't overtop it to wash through the jetty like they had at this time last year.

By the time the tide turned the beach had grown a foot higher and ten feet further seaward. I remembered seeing this happen on Cape Cod when the beach grew a berm that was 6 feet high and over 30 feet wide because of long period waves from a hurricane that was hundreds of miles away. Sometimes beaches can grow as much as a hundred feet on a single tidal cycle under such conditions.

I made my way back along the jetty path that had also been damaged by the recent storm. Sand had washed through the boulders in the jetty leaving 3-foot deep sinkholes in the path. I decided to take the upper path where I could see the waves sliding up the steep face of the beach and tearing away dune grass in front of the houses along Northern Reservation Terrace.

But what I didn't see were any 14-foot high artificial sand dunes, like those I had seen along the Jersey Coast. These dunes had been built 14 feet above sea level, not 14 feet above ground level. The state had only paid enough to fill in the low spots with a few feet of sand, so the whole dune field was only about 14 feet above sea level. This did not seem very auspicious. Waves were already tearing away plugs of dune grass that had been planted along the face of the dune.

But the real problem was that the 10-foot high king tides would return in just two weeks. What would happen if they coincided with a modest storm with 8-foot high waves like we had just experienced, or a storm with 20-foot waves like we had last winter? We would have to see...

CHAPTER 17
Reflections
December 12, 2016

It was difficult to tell the artificial dune from the natural dune. It was truly a piece of installation art.

On December 12, I went out to North Point to see how the beach had fared during the recent king tide. So far, so good. It was the first day of an eight-day stretch of over nine foot high tides.

It was flat calm. Just cool green waters sliding along the riverside beach. If the weather stayed like this we would be fine. But this was early winter in New England where we hardly ever get eight days of good weather.

I made my way along the seaward dune of the newly completed dual dune system. It certainly looked better than a week ago when eight-foot waves were sliding up the beach face.

The jetty was a different story. The long period waves were a foot and a half, hardly high enough to be seen offshore, but they still packed enough power to move sand around when they rose up and broke on the beach.

When we see waves breaking on the shore we usually think they are eroding the beach. But these waves were building the beach. Sand was flowing north on the longshore currents until it ran into waves refracting off the jetty.

They had created a countercurrent flowing south and together the two currents were colluding to build a three-foot high point of sand that jutted about 20 feet into the ocean. I watched as wave after wave washed up and over the point, leaving a wrackline that had darker and heavier shells than the surrounding sand.

Usually the waves were too chaotic to reveal this pattern, but in these calm conditions they provided more than enough energy to build up this small point of sand. But it happened almost every day with waves building this point higher and higher and welding it to the growing beach. It was also the reason that there was a ridge of sand almost five feet higher than the jetty about 20 feet back from the jetty but not pushed up against the jetty itself. This was part of the reserve of sand that would flow through the jetty during a major storm.

From the jetty I walked back through the dunes. It allowed me to look at the new dunes more carefully. Workers had driven in snow fencing along the paths and roped off the front of the dunes, so people wouldn't trample down the newly planted dune grass. The low dunes blended in with the natural dunes so well that it was difficult to tell them apart. It was a work of art, but hopefully not a just a temporary installation piece.

Chapter 18
The Party
December 10, 2016

Fracking.

In early December, I went to a party near Plum Island. Inevitably the conversation pivoted from how could the democrats have ever lost to Donald Trump, to his picks for the EPA, the Department of Interior and Secretary of State; then on to the protest de jour of East Coast liberals, the anti-fracking encampment in Standing Rock North Dakota.

It occurred to me that all these issues were related. It was difficult to find anyone on either the East or West coasts that had anything good to say about fracking. Why would anyone want to do something that caused earthquakes, polluted water and increased methane emissions?

But for people in red states, fracking is often an entryway into the American dream. In what other industry could someone with a high school education start out earning $66,000 and expect a salary of between $100,00 to $200,000 with a little more time and education? It was one of the few manufacturing industries where you could still get a decent foothold in the middle class.

Who cared about a few little earthquakes? Do folks leave California because of earthquakes? Do people leave Florida because salt water has intruded into their water supply? No they just buy bottled water. And who knows what methane emissions are anyway? Don't they have something to do with cow flatulence?

But, with the nomination of Rex Tillerson as Secretary of State and Scott Pruitt as head of the EPA, it was clear that our foreign and domestic policies were going to switch to an oil based worldview emanating out of Texas, not Washington or even New York. That worldview sees national power as coming not so much from democratic ideals and institutions but from access to cheap energy.

People living on the East and West coasts don't really understand this petroleum-centric worldview but it is in the very genes of people like Rex Tillerson who has spent his entire career working for the oil industry.

When Tillerson took over as CEO of Exxon Mobile, the company's future looked bleak indeed. They were hemorrhaging cash and rapidly losing their position as the largest oil company in the world because they had missed out on the fracking boom. They got into the business too late and had bought an overpriced fracking company called XTO.

But small-scale fracking had never been Exxon Mobile's style. They had always relied on superior technology and vast amounts of capital to exploit oil fields that no other company, or country, could afford to pursue.

But Tillerson soon found a willing partner in Russia that was running out of its own reserves of easily exploitable oil. He teamed up with the Russian oil company Rostneft to drill in the Black Sea and to develop Russia's Siberian shale fields, but most of all to explore Russia's big enchilada, their Arctic oil fields beneath the Kara Sea.

Tillerson had to beat out both Chevron and BP to make a deal with Russia to invest $3.2 billion to develop the Kara Sea oil fields that reportedly held more oil and gas than all the fields in the Gulf of Mexico combined.

Vladimir Putin personally gave Tillerson Russia's Order of Friendship medal for Exxon's part of the deal. It was this that convinced Trump that Tillerson would be a better dealmaker than either Mitt Romney or Rudolf Giuliani.

But right after the Exxon Rostneft partnership struck oil with Tillerson on board the drill ship, Putin invaded Ukraine and Hillary Clinton placed sanctions on Russia under President Obama's orders. The sanctions meant that Exxon had to stop using it's technology to continue drilling for oil in the Kara Sea.

Tillerson was appalled that the Obama would put the lives and freedom of people in Ukraine before the strategic interest of getting our hands on Russian oil. His counterpart Igor Sechin, the president of Rostneft, was equally appalled at Putin for inviting the sanctions by invading the Ukraine. They agreed that their respective leaders knew bupkis about business.

But what about the ramifications of drilling all that Arctic oil for climate change? Not really on Tillerson's radar screen. He knew it was real but he also knew oil meant national power and economic expansion.

Tillerson might actually make an effective Secretary of State and would probably push to remove the sanctions on Russia. Trump had already tipped his hand that was in the cards. From a hard-nosed petroleum-centric point of view this could even be good for the American and Russian positions in the world. It just might not be very good for people in the former Soviet satellites or for the future of our planet.

CHAPTER 19
A Trojan Horse on the Trump Estate?
Rex Tillerson
December 28, 2016

Offshore oil rig Galveston Texas.

As 2016 sputtered down to an uninspiring end, Plum Island continued to enjoy an almost unprecedented spate of calm weather. There had been no significant storms in either the fall or early winter. But the calm spell had given me time to continue reflecting on Donald Trump's selection for Secretary of State, who might soon be in charge of seeing that the United States adheres to the Paris climate change accords and works for world stability.

The more I looked at Rex Tillerson, the more I thought some of my colleagues in the environmental movement were barking up the wrong tree. For example, I posted an article that showed how Henry Kissinger had met Vladimir Putin early in the young KGB agent's career and explained that Kissinger hoped to use that connection to work with Tillerson. I thought it was a fascinating insider's glimpse of how personal diplomacy is actually conducted in the real world. But the piece evoked the response that all three men were fascists of the same feather.

Fascists, really? Someone whose family had fled Europe to escape the Nazis? Someone who had been an avowed communist? Someone who had worked his way up through the engineering ranks to become head of the largest oil company in the world?

But the thing that made me first realize that Tillerson might not be so bad was a quote from Massachusetts Senator Elizabeth Warren who said she had received a letter from an old law school friend who was married to Tillerson. She assured Warren that Tillerson would make a thoughtful Secretary of State. If one of the most liberal Senators in Congress was willing to give Tillerson another look, shouldn't I do the same?

I also remembered that when Tillerson took over as the CEO of Exxon Mobile one of the first things he did was to appoint a committee to look into Exxon's policies on climate change. Then he announced that climate change was real and directed his executives to start cutting funding to organizations that denied climate change. More recently he had come out in favor of the Paris Climate Accords.

Exxon's many executives and scientists heralded these moves as a long overdue. They had grown weary of Exxon's former CEO, Lee Raymond's personal beliefs that climate change was just a concocted hoax.

Then I read an eloquent letter to the editor in the Dallas Times. It was written by Emily Roden who described her experience sitting on a jury in the Denton County Court House.

"Perhaps it was the middle-aged man's business suit, perhaps it was his impressive stature or charisma but almost everyone in that jury room felt this man was the best person to be our foreman. But he declined, saying simply, 'I'm not interested in the spotlight.'"

During a break, Roden was busily checking on her e-mails and remarked to the mystery man how much work she had to do. He just smiled and went back to reading his newspaper.

But from that first day everyone on, the jury noticed another man who sat in room and always had an earpiece jammed in his ear. During lunch breaks the two men would sit together and talk quietly. The two mystery men became the object of the entire jury's curiosity.

Finally one of the jury members screwed up his nerve and asked, "Just who are you and what do you do?"

The mystery man pointed to an article about Exxon Mobile and said, "I work for them and there are a lot of people who hate me for what I do, so they give me and my family big guys like these to protect us."

Roden's face reddened as she remembered complaining about how much work she had to do and it didn't take her too many Internet searches before she realized she was sitting beside Rex Tillerson.

The case they were deciding involved a young girl who had been sexually assaulted by her mother's boyfriend. The majority of the jurists were convinced of the sex offender's guilt but defense had done a good enough job that there were two holdouts.

That was when Tillerson began to speak. "Very humbly and delicately, without an ounce of condescension he walked us through the details of the case. With patience this man who strikes multimillion dollar deals with foreign heads of state brought our scrappy jury together—to bring a sexual predator to justice and to deliver justice to a scared and deeply wounded little girl."

A local non-profit agency had been helping the young girl throughout the process. Emily had been so struck by the group's mission that she toured their facility and made a small donation to their cause.

On a whim she e-mailed Tillerson to ask him to do the same. To her surprise she received an e-mail right back thanking her for her note, and her jury duty, and ensuring her that he would contact the agency.

A few days later the director of the group called to tell her that Tillerson had followed through with a generous contribution. He also had Exxon contribute to Planned Parenthood. Not the moves of a hard-core social conservative, but the moves of a non-ideological problem solver.

All of these stories plus the fact that Tillerson's name had been given to Trump by two of George Bush's former Secretaries of State, Condoleezza Rice and James Baker, made me think that Tillerson might prove to be one of the only sane voices in Trump's entire cabinet, a Trojan horse who might counter his boss's penchant for tweets and unpredictability.

Plus, if there is one thing that oil companies have always been good at, it has been thinking far into the future and supporting policies to make the world stable, for their long-term investments if nothing else. That will be crucial if we are to make it though the next decade. And the next decade will be crucial for the future of our planet.

CHAPTER 20
The Chatham Connection
January 3, 2017

Chatham Inlet. It could happen on Plum Island.

January 3 was a warm, blustery day. Ten-foot waves from last night's storm were breaking over the shoals beyond the Merrimack River. I could just make out a medium-sized boat caught in the maelstrom. She was plunging and bucking into waves that were exploding all around her. Each wave would send a twenty foot geyser of freezing water into the air, then cascade down on four men clad in survival suits who hung on for dear life. But suddenly the boat broke free and made a dash for the quiet waters inside the jetties.

There, I could see she was one of the Coast Guard's 47-foot shallow draft boats first used in Chatham Harbor. She was soon joined by another life saving boat and after reconnoitering for a bit they sped back into the waves. Were they looking for an overturned fishing boat, or the body of a fisherman swept out to sea?

Nah, they were just on a training exercise putting some newbie Coastie through his paces in the mouth of what the Coast Guard calls the most dangerous river on the East Coast. In fact Newburyport is the birthplace of the U.S. Coast Guard. Alexander Hamilton started it here before Lin Manuel Miranda made him into a 21st century hip hop star, "Our river was so treacherous, we tole the Brits don't mess wid us."

Having gotten that out of my system, I went to see how North Beach had weathered the storm. All things considered it had done very well. Last night's waves had only eroded a few feet off the face of the temporary new dune built to protect the houses along Northern Reservation Terrace.

But other waves had washed over the dune delivering a new layer of sand that would stimulate the dune grass to grow an internal matrix of roots and rhizomes to hold the dune together. So the sacrificial dune was doing its job, absorbing the waves' energy while building a barrier to slow future erosion.

However, things were different on the jetty. For the past four months, long period waves had built up a ridge of sand that blocked less powerful waves from crashing through the jetty. But last night's storm had flattened the ridge protecting the last 204 feet of the jetty. So future waves could now be able to wash sand through the jetty again. Several thousands cubic yards had washed through just last night.

The storm reminded me of a similar storm that struck Chatham, Massachusetts on exactly the same day 30 years before. The storm and its ensuing inlet caused seismic changes to the town and they continue to plague the town today. If a storm breaks through Plum Island it could cause similar changes to Newburyport, Newbury, Rowley and Ipswich, so it makes sense to see exactly what happened on Cape Cod.

It was not that the storm was particularly strong, but that it arrived at exactly the wrong time. The barrier beach that protects Chatham had been growing longer and lower for several years and it had not been helped by boaters who made a habit of walking over the low dunes to get to the ocean beach.

That was exactly where the 12 foot high storm surge burst through the beach on a full moon when the sun, moon and earth were all in line, a so-called syzygy tide. The next morning people awoke to a new reality, but it was not terribly impressive one, just a foot deep channel meandering back and forth through an overwash area the size of a football field.

Ten guys with shovels could have filled the break back in on that first low tide, but they didn't and only a month later the channel was over 18 feet deep and commercial fishermen were using it to cut an hour off the trip to their fishing grounds. But, since nobody had expected an inlet to form, nobody had come up with a plan to fill it back in.

But the inlet really shouldn't have taken anyone by surprise. Unlike on Plum Island, a prominent scientist had predicted when the inlet would open in a classic piece of shoe leather coastal geology. Graham Giese, one of the founders of the Provincetown Center for Coastal Geology had detailed a 140 year cycle where the lengthening barrier beach would cause hydraulic pressure to build up in Pleasant Bay until a storm broke through the barrier beach. Then the southern part of the beach would weld to the mainland allowing the northern part to grow until it broke in exactly the same place — 140 years later.

But because Graham was a correctly conservative scientist he had rounded his cycle off to 150 years. I liked to chide him that if he had stuck to his guns he would have only been two days off because the new inlet had formed on January 2nd. 1987.

Despite Graham's paper everyone had been taken by surprise. It had been a long time since the last inlet formed in 1846. So long that people had forgotten why they called their barrier beach North Beach when it wasn't really north of anything. But as soon as the new inlet opened they realized they now had a North Beach and South Beach like back in 1846.

Prior to the storm Chathamites, like Newburyporters, thought they lived behind a permanent barrier..Everyone had always assumed that the fishing camps on the outer beach were vulnerable, but nobody realized how much damage the inlet could do to the mainland. They were disabused of that notion when ocean waves started to sweep houses off the mainland for the first time in over a hundred years.

Homeowners had to spend millions of dollars to build several miles of revetments and the Army Corps of Engineers had to spend hundreds of thousands of dollars to dredge the new sand out of Chatham Harbor.

Pleasant Bay had become 6 inches higher at high tide and 6 inches lower at low tide and houses like ours, 12 miles from the inlet, had started experiencing erosion for the first time in memory. The bay had experienced the equivalent of 50 years of sea level rise overnight.

Thirty years later another inlet formed and a dozen camps were lost on the outer beach. Then a third inlet formed and it will still take one to three decades for the system to fully stabilize.

Similar things could happen if the ocean breaks through Plum Island. If it breaks through on the southern end of the island, streets and homes in Ipswich could be affected. If it breaks through in the middle of the island, streets and homes in Rowley and Newbury could also eventually be affected. But if it breaks through on the north end of Plum Island, Plum Bush, Joppa Flats, The Basin, and even houses on Water Street in Newburyport could be lost.

Plum Island still lacked a study equivalent to what Graham Geise produced for the Chatham Conservation Commission. It was still relying on local hearsay and less than rigorous research done in the Seventies with outdated technology. That would start to change when the Merrimack Valley Regional Planning Authority released its Woods Hole study on sediment transport and when the Army Corps released two similar studies. Hopefully they would get it right and they would all agree!

CHAPTER 21
Green Crabs and Bonfires
January 14, 2017

Cooked Green Crab with roe.

Tension was heavy as our nation counted down toward Donald's Trump's January 20th Inaugural. While Rex Tillerson's confirmation hearings were carried out with relative dignity, Trump's first press conference devolved into a frightening yelling match. Then local advertisements started blaring, "burn baby burn" to advertise the town of Newbury's annual burning of a 3-story high pile of Christmas trees.

Was this the right message to be sending when we were experiencing climate change induced drought from so much carbon dioxide being released into the atmosphere? Average citizens couldn't even burn leaves in the fall, but it was OK for the town to build a huge bonfire to burn Christmas trees for a spectacle that would only last 30 minutes? I figured the bonfire had to be some sort of atavistic tradition that went back to the Fifties.

But someone had dreamed up this tone-deaf celebration the same time that Plum Island's houses were tumbling into the surf due to climate change. Had the tradition been started out of ignorance or in defiance? That "burn, baby burn" with its evocations of urban riots and calls for the unfettered drilling of oil sure made it sound like the latter.

I had been planning to go to the bonfire to see for myself. But fortunately, January was also the time when fishermen start to prepare for their upcoming season and I had been invited to join a fascinating group of people hoping to start up a soft-shelled green crab industry in nearby Ipswich.

It was a cold, crisp, clear morning when I joined the convoy of trucks and cars from New Hampshire, Maine and Massachusetts wending their way along a dirt road beside the mouth of the Essex River estuary. Rafts of salt marsh hay lay in the road strewn there by last night's king tide.

After about a mile we arrived at a dock and the organizer of the symposium, Roger Warner, explained that this was one of the spots where fishermen might land and sort their catch.

The Ipswich shellfish warden, Scott La Preste, explained the problem. Every year the town usually landed about 80,000 pounds of soft-shelled clams or steamers. But recently the town's shellfish beds had been threatened by green crabs, an invasive species from Northern Europe. Ipswich had set up a program to encourage fishermen to trap the crabs and sell them for bait. But if you could market the crabs as a delicacy item you would solve two problems. One way to do that would be to sell the crabs as soft-shelled, the way blue crabs were sold in Louisiana and the Chesapeake. But that was easier said than done.

The pugnacious little crabs had established a foothold in Canada then spread south, so Canadians had more time to figure something out. Sophie St. Hillaire, a pioneering marine biologist from Prince Edward Island, explained to the group how she had set up two systems to identify and hold crabs until they shed their shells in the early spring. She taught her own young children how to distinguish the subtle signs that indicate when a crab was about to molt. Then she made daily observations of the crabs that she held both in floating pens in the wild and in an indoor lab where she could control their ambient water temperature.

She rewarded her children with ice cream cones and they became so adept at identifying the molting crabs that she had elevated her kids' status to interns in her annual scientific reports.

Jonathan Taggart showed slides of the Moeche fishery in Venice. He was an art preservationist whose professional work often brought him to Venice, where he had discovered the artisanal soft-shelled green crab fishery. He explained that the magnifying glasses he used in his preservation work helped him identify the subtle signs of a pre-molt soft-shelled crab or *Moeche*.

He received highest accolades from the Venetian fishermen who said that all of the specimens he had sorted out with his specialized glasses were *grancia buono*, good crabs.

Jonathan lived in Maine and passed this information on to several neighboring shell fishermen who were interested in starting up their own soft-shelled crab businesses. Two of them had also driven down to attend the symposium.

By the end of the day the group had a plan. Kevin Cheung, a fisherman and aquaculturist from southern Massachusetts would start trapping the crabs when the water temperatures started to rise above 50 degrees in March. He would then contact about half a dozen Ipswich fishermen who sold green crabs to fishermen from the mid-Atlantic who used the crabs as bait to catch conch, tautog and eel for the sushi industry. They had also expanded their business to selling crabs to Boston restaurants that had started to serve green crab broth.

Then the word would go out to the New Hampshire Sea Grant program and to the fishermen in Maine. And through trial and error, this eclectic mix of fishermen, marine biologists, government officials, marketing specialists and seafood writers would make it all work.

Their idea was that trapping the crabs for bait would be their core business that would both protect the clam-flats and support the sushi industry. But during the early spring months, Ipswich fishermen, along with biologists, interns and volunteers would learn how to identify the pre-molting crabs then separate and hold the crabs until they molted and could be marketed as soft-shelled crabs.

Restaurants and wholesalers had already told marketing specialists that they would buy as many soft-shelled green crabs as Ipswich could produce and sell them for $6 to $8 a pound. Not a bad business model, now they just had to see if it would work.

CHAPTER 22
Our First Bona Fide Northeaster
January 25, 2017

Results of the first Northeaster of 2017.

On January 25, I lay in bed listening to the season's first bona fide Northeaster. I knew the wind was gusting over 50 miles per hour because our chimney cap starts to roar when the wind tops that speed.

We were in the waning hours of a storm that had raged for the last 48 hours; with snow, rain, wind and 18-foot waves that had pounded the shore for the last four tidal cycles.

I had been planning to take photographs during the 9:25am high tide, but since it was 5:00 in the morning and I couldn't sleep anyway, I decided it made more sense to get up and make it to Plum Island before the sun. That would give me three hours to walk on the beach before the high tide hemmed me in against the duneline.

So I grabbed my gear and set out in the drizzling rain. I arrived at Center Groin just before sunrise to find two photographers already there. One of them had to be my friend Jim Fenton. This was just his time of day and weather. But I wanted to see how the houses in Newbury had fared, so I turned right and headed up Southern Boulevard.

Suddenly I saw projectile sized rocks and pieces of tar strewn across the street. The owner of the adjacent lot had been using the rocks to fill in chinks in the seawall in front of his house, but last night's waves had blasted the rocks off the seawall and washed them down a gully beside his house. This had left ocean water standing on the public road where the island's primary water and sewer mains were buried.

The waves had undermined the seawall causing the foundation of the house to crack. The same thing had happened in 2014, 2015 and 2016.

Waves had also washed through an empty lot on Fordham Way knocking down a sign offering the property for sale, and waves had splashed over the Center Groin area. This had been where the Army Corps of Engineers had constructed a berm to prevent the island from breaking in two almost a decade before.

It was still drizzling and overcast as I drove north to see how the temporary sand dune in Newburyport's end of the island had fared. It was still about three hours before high tide, but waves were already nibbling at the base of the sacrificial dune.

But yesterday's waves had overtopped the dune, eroding it back ten feet and allowing overwash to come within 40 paces of the nearest house on Northern Reservation Terrace. At this rate, waves could be licking at the foundations of his neighbors' homes in three months. And if the ocean broke through Northern Reservation Terrace, the Merrimack River could potentially find a new outlet to the ocean, isolating up to 250 homes. The only long-term remedy lay on top of South Jetty, my next stop.

The wind blasted my face as I crested the dunes. Eight-foot waves were still slamming into the jetty from both sides. Ocean waves were already washing sand through a 50-foot stretch of the jetty. But I could see that during last night's high tide, they had been washing through the jetty for almost 320 feet, probably enough to wash half an acre of sand through the jetty. Last year water flowed through the entire thousand-foot length of the jetty, depositing an acre of sand four feet deep during every winter month.

The jetty also revealed another interesting phenomenon. There was a 5-foot deep sinkhole about three feet from the jetty. Last night water had rushed down through the hole and out through the jetty. But something else was going on as well. I could hear water gurgling through the bottom of the sinkhole. This meant that waves were washing freely through the jetty from both sides. This had already caused the jetty to settle almost three feet in the last three years. If it continued, enough sand would be able to flow through the jetty to rebuild the beach and protect the houses on Northern Reservation Terrace.

But it had to happen fast. The entire face of the beach had retreated back 40 feet since April, including ten feet in just the past two days. Water had also come within 20 paces of a beach gazebo at the end of North Point. At that rate waves could overtop the dunes and flood across the parking lot to where the water and sewer mains were buried under Northern Boulevard.

But when I came off the beach, I was surprised by a large new green sign welcoming people to Newburyport's Plum Island Beach. Finally this beach had a name. For years nobody knew who owned the beach and what to call it. This simple but eloquent sign was a signal that local people took pride in this beautiful beach and next summer's visitors would hopefully follow their example.

CHAPTER 23
A First Piece of Solid Science
February 3, 2017

Stippled area shows erosion after Jetty repair. Courtesy Mike Morris.

"We've gone a long way by the seat of our pants," was how Senator Bruce Tarr summed up the last 40 years of making decisions about Plum Island without adequate science.

But that era ended when coastal geologists, Matt Shultz and Bob Hamilton from the Woods Hole Group, presented their sediment transport analysis at the monthly meeting of the Merrimack River Beach Alliance on February 3, 2017.

It was a game changing study, a study that exploded the convenient myths that decision makers had been using to justify things like building groins, seawalls and repairing jetties that had all clearly increased the natural rate of erosion on the island which was only two feet a year.

For decades people had been using the simplistic myth that the dominant sand moving current flowed south along the entire length of Plum Island. This notion had been extrapolated from research done in the Seventies that used old wind rose data to say that the waves that formed those currents blew predominantly from the Northeast.

But the Woods Hole Group used wind and wave data from modern offshore oceanographic buoys. They showed that 95% of the time, waves hit Plum Island from the East and the East South East and it was only during those few days during Northeasters that waves hit the shore from the Northeast. The data they used was from a fifty-year storm, which gives an indication how seldom this occurs.

So 95% of the time, waves hit the island and split at a node in the undeveloped center of the island on National Wildlife property. Then they create currents that flow both from the center of the island north and from the center of the island south.

During a Northeaster however, this node could move north to raise havoc with houses in the developed part of the island. This was particularly damaging where you had something like a groinfield that not only interfered with the beneficial flow of sand north during calm periods but also focused the energy of waves on houses behind the groinfield during storms. It is noteworthy that all the houses that had been lost in the last nine years had been immediately downstream of these groins.

Since the island was eroding at the rate of 2 feet a year, you could expect a house sitting on the edge of the dunes in the center of the island to be lost within twenty years, but you could expect a house sitting on end of the island which was growing to last for decades longer.

The scientists also showed a graphic of the north end of the island just before the repair work on the South Jetty had been completed in 2014. It showed bright red areas of erosion above the jetty and bright blue areas of accretion or growth below the jetty. It was this sand that was flowing through the jetty that had been protecting the houses on Northern Reservation Terrace for the past 217 years.

A FIRST PIECE OF SOLID SCIENCE

But we knew that once the jetty had been repaired, the situation had reversed. Sand had grown 304 feet seaward above the jetty, while over 300 feet of dunes and beach had eroded below the jetty.

This set up a perfect experiment. If they ran the model showing that the newly repaired jetty was now trapping sand instead of letting it through, all the areas that had been red would turn blue and all the areas that had been blue would turn red. It would be a little like watching television the night Trump was elected.

CHAPTER 24
Three Storms in February
February 7, February 9, February 13

Old Coast Guard Station. This pole first jutted out of the dune in February 2016. The scarp eroded back 15 feet in less than a year. This pole fell the day after this shot was taken.

We had three little storms in early February. They all packed 20 mile per hour winds and had about 5 or 6-foot waves riding on top of 8 or 9-foot high tides. They were exactly what you would expect during the winter months in New England. In fact you could call them one-week storms.

But it was the cumulative nature of these storms that caused so much damage. They just hammered the shore; storm, after storm, after storm.

On February 8th, I drove out to North Point to see the results of the first storm. It was a bright sunny day with temperatures close to 50 degrees. When I arrived at low tide I walked out the 69th street path that led to the temporary dune. It had continued doing its sacrificial job.

Most of the dune was gone, leaving a dangerous six foot drop to the beach. It was impassable, but I could see where someone had lifted his heavy dog up from the beach to the dune where it had clawed away several inches of sand, not the end of the world mind you, but also not something you wanted done if your house was being protected by that dune.

The dune had been cut off so sharply you could see plugs of dune grass in exactly the same condition as when they had been planted in early December. They hadn't had enough time to root. The state probably should have waited for the winter erosion season to be over before planting on what was left of the dune. But it was a process of live and learn.

I could also see where waves had washed over the primary dune and come within 40 feet of the closest house on Northern Reservation Terrace. But what interested me most were marks in the sand below the remains of the old coast guard station. It looked like someone had dug a large trench at the bottom of the twenty-foot high cliff.

Since the path was so scarped, I had to go out to the jetty then return on a lower path that sloped gradually to the beach. But the detour allowed me to see that waves had pushed the acre-sized fillet of sand that had flowed through the jetty during the January 24th storm about a hundred feet further along the jetty. It would take about two weeks more for that sandbar to snake its way around the spur of the jetty, so it could then protect the south end of Plum Island Beach.

Interestingly enough, the sandbar held about 6,000 cubic yards of sand, which was about 4 times more sand than what the state had used to build both dunes. So that sand could potentially be available if they decided to rebuild the dunes.

But the big surprise came when I walked beneath the old coast guard station; a 15-foot piece of its parking lot had collapsed along with about 50 linear feet of the dune itself.

It looked like it had collapsed only hours before. Sand was still sliding down the vertical scarp, searching for its angle of repose. It did not bode well for future storms.

Most people thought the second storm had been more powerful because it had packed stronger winds, created whiteout conditions and dropped over seven inches of snow. But that storm had developed quickly on February 9th, and then arrived near low tide before raging on toward Canada.

The storm had also been so close to the coast that its waves only arrived as 4 or 5-foot short period waves rather than the larger more powerful long period waves that can develop when a storm is further offshore.

When I drove out to see the results of this second storm, the winds were still howling and the temperature had plummeted to a frigid 19 degrees with a minus four degree wind chill factor. Snow had drifted so high on the first path I tried that I had to turn back and try another, which put me further down the beach. But it was low tide so I could walk below the dunes.

During the previous night's high tide, the Merrimack River had lifted great rafts of salt marsh hay off the upper marshes and deposited it in long windrows along Plum Island Beach. They had formed barriers that had helped prevent waves from overtopping the dunes and running down paths toward people's Northern Reservation Terrace homes. But the waves had been able to continue under-mining the dunes, so they had eroded back several more feet.

The erosion was most apparent below the old coast guard station. The 15-foot piece of the parking lot that had been made up of unconsolidated gravel had completely washed away. If I hadn't come across it immediately after it had collapsed when I was out here two days before, I never would have known what had happened. All that was left was the steep sandy cliff where the piece of parking lot had been before. The ocean has a way of covering its tracks after committing such transgressions.

But it was simply too cold and windy to continue out to the jetty. So I decided to punt. The third storm was on the way but I had made previous plans to go to Florida. I didn't want to miss anything but if it was a choice between lying in the sun in Florida or experiencing yet another New England storm, I was more than happy to take my chances in Florida. After all what could possibly go wrong during a single week in February?

CHAPTER 25
Cayo Costa, Florida
February 21, 2017

Cayo Costa.

My vacation would allow me to see how Florida would fare in the present era of rising seas and stronger more frequent storms. My informant for these explorations would be John Martin, an old friend from high school who now lived in Punta Gorda, near Fort Meyers.

Our trip started out on Cayo Costa, a barrier beach island on Florida's West Coast. My family had a longstanding relationship with this island. My father brought me to the island thirty years before, and when we found the scale of a tarpon with his father's initials on it in a nearby bar he remembered the day my grandfather had caught it. Not because of the fish. But because my grandmother had been so ticked at my grandfather for returning home several sheets to windward. Those were in the days when you went down to Boca Grande by train and stayed for the full season at the gracious Gasparilla Inn.

Unlike nearby Sanibel and Captiva islands, no bridge or revetments had ever been built on Cayo Costa. This had left the island able to fulfill its function as a natural barrier against major storms, so people could live safely behind the barrier beaches as the Callussa Indians had done hundreds of years before. The lack of houses and infrastructure made it easier for Florida to make the island into a state park in 1971.

The wisdom of that effort had been tested when Hurricane Charley arrived on August 13, 2004. After passing over Key West as a Category 3 hurricane, Charley had suddenly turned northeast and increased to a category 5 hurricane before smashing over Cayo Costa and on into Punta Gorda area where it caused $15 billion in damages and left hundreds of people living in FEMA trailers years after the storm had passed.

But Cayo Costa looked much as I remembered it 30 years before, and probably much like it looked five hundred years before that. Tendrils of fog lifted slowly along its nine miles of powdery white beaches. However, all the Australian pine trees I remembered towering over the island had been snapped in two. Park rangers had spent years trying to remove the invasive trees by chain saw, before Charley did it for them in ten minutes, flat.

Now copses of native sea grapes were thriving in the sunlight where the pines used to be. But the wild boar that used to emerge from native Palmetto palm groves to root for mole crabs on the tidal flats and the feral horses that used to nuzzle visiting boaters seemed to be gone. But alligators still lurked in the shallow lagoon just behind the swimming beach. And of course the productive waters of the Gulf of Mexico still produced billions of shells that washed up on the deceptively quiet beaches of Cayo Costa – deceptive because they still remained ready to absorb the powers of the next hurricane. They reflected the benefit of leaving a barrier beach in its natural state to stave off future storms. And the best way to do that was to make it into a public park.

And now the park was thriving. Every day hundreds of visitors arrived in their own boats or on small ferries and would be taken across the island in modified golf carts driven by park volunteers. There they could spread out along a seven-mile long pristine white Gulf of Mexico beach, or pitch a tent and spend the week fishing.

If you looked carefully you could see where the beach had rolled over itself as it moved inland during hurricane Charley and you could see some areas of slight erosion. But you never read anything about erosion on Cayo Costa because it had no houses or streets to wash away. So the island just remains a natural barrier island, ready to protect the mainland from the next hurricane.

We hoped to compare Cayo Costa to a built up barrier beach on the hurricane prone Atlantic Coast of Florida. We scrutinized the map and found the perfect location 200 miles directly east. It happened to be Mar-a-Lago, President Trump's winter white house on tony Palm Beach. We wondered if they would admit two old geezers from New England. Perhaps we could mention we knew Bill Bellichick.

CHAPTER 26
Mar-a-Lago
February 23, 2017

Trump door; Entrance to Mar-a-Lago.

After visiting Cayo Costa, John had taken us by boat to Cabbage Key. Cabbage Key and its sister island, Useppa, are unique archaeological sites. Estuaries are the only ecosystems that are biologically productive enough to be able to support large year round populations of humans without resorting to agriculture.

This made life easy for the Callussa people because they didn't have to build irrigation canals or do any hard agricultural labor. But their leaders took care of that. They organized the Callussas into unpaid work gangs to build step pyramids like those built by the Mayans in Mexico. The pyramids were located on the many keys that lay protected behind the string of barrier beaches that included Sanibel, Captiva and Gasparilla Islands.

The Callusas hafted wooden handles onto the Lightning Whelks that proliferated in the area and used the heavy shells as grub hoes to build the pyramids. They used the whelks once again to cover the pyramids with abstract whorled patterns. Then they built a series of canals so their scouts could scoot from behind the barrier islands to the pyramids to warn of danger. This proved useful when Spanish explorers started snooping around their kingdom in the 1600's.

Today the remains of these step pyramids and their extensive shell middens are the highest points in Southwest Florida—all that is left of their leaders' overweening egos and taste in monuments to themselves.

We were reminded of that as we drove across Florida to visit Mar-a-Lago. My original plan was to simply take a few pictures of the Italianate villa that sits only 4 feet above sea level on our country's most hurricane prone shore. But that was before I realized that the President intended to run his shambolic administration from his imperial looking villa every weekend.

So we didn't really know what to expect. I told John I would be more than happy if we could just took a few pictures from the car. Even if we were turned away, I could probably write a story about the expensive security surrounding our president who has residences in New York, Washington, New Jersey and Florida.

We had planned to park at a nearby island and take pictures across the bayou but the bridge to Palm Beach was open so we decided to see if we could drive by the villa itself.

No security was in sight, so we drove down a side street where a cop car was parked. We figured we could ask if it was OK to take a few photographs but the car was empty so we parked and walked.

The adjacent street was separated from Mar-a-Lago by a high hedge and trees but a path led through the vegetation to an open gate. I took a few steps down the path and took a photograph of a huge American flag flapping over the red-tiled building. A couple explained that the city of Palm Beach had tried to restrict the height of the oversized flag but had been overridden -- by executive order no doubt.

Since nobody was around I took a few more steps and suddenly realized I was almost inside the compound itself. A groundskeeper eventually came along and explained that this was a private resort and that we would have to leave. We said we were sorry and walked back to our car.

Nobody had bothered to ask for credentials or just what exactly we thought we were doing. Even though the President wasn't in residence we were shocked at the lack of security.

But I suppose if I were President Trump I would be far less concerned about two old geezers with cameras than section 4 of the Constitution's 25th amendment. That's the one that empowers a majority of the principal officers of the executive departments to declare the President unfit for office and to install the Vice President in his stead.

It was fascinating to see how a little short-term problem like a political or consti-tutional crisis could draw your attention away from a long-term problem like sea level rise. I wonder if the Calussas ever noticed the same thing?

CHAPTER 27
Beach Paths and Mobi-mats
March 2, 2017

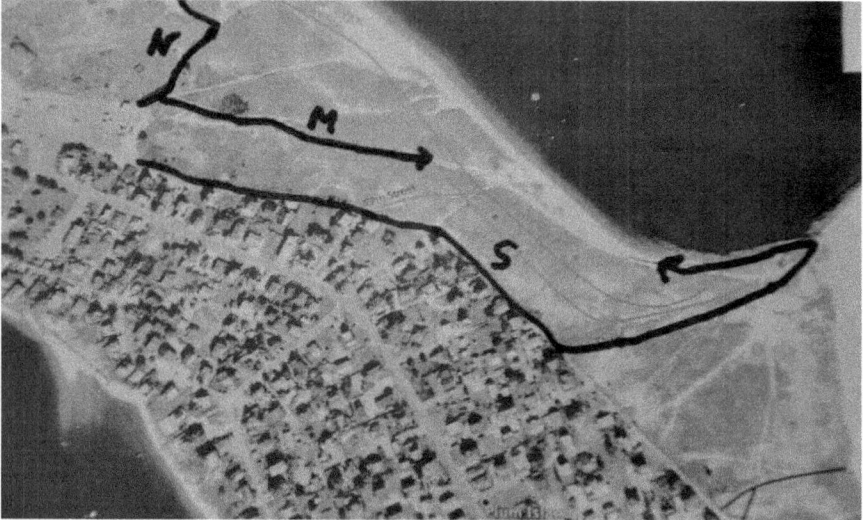

Suggested paths, Plum Island Beach.

By March 2, 2017 I had returned from Florida to attend a meeting funded by Massachusetts Coastal Zone Management to decide where to put portable boardwalks called mobi-mats on Plum Island Beach. Participants drew straws to sit at five different tables with aerial maps of the beach. Because the beach had been neglected so long, it was crisscrossed with a network of redundant paths. Many of the paths seemed to have been only used for a few weeks one summer, before being abandoned.

Each table was composed of residents, fishing enthusiasts and members of groups like the Massachusetts Beach Buggy Association. We were asked to select three paths that could be eliminated and some that should be saved.

After 15 minutes of discussion each table presented their results. It was instructive how much agreement there was between participants. All the tables felt that between 13 and 17 paths could be eliminated and only a few left open.

I came away from the exercise thinking that it was only necessary to have three main paths to the beach; one along the existing boardwalk, one to the center of the beach and one from Northern Reservation Terrace to the jetty.

The North Path

During the Fall, waves had eroded 30 feet off the dunes to the right of boardwalk that runs from the North End parking lot to the beach. The sand had been deposited about seventy feet to the left of the boardwalk where the beach grew a hundred feet.

So it would make sense to have beachgoers walk down the existing boardwalk, jog left, then continue for about seventy feet on a mobi-mat, before entering the beach where it has been growing about fifteen feet a month since October. The rest of the beach had eroded about twenty feet since the fall. The idea was to shift people from entering the beach where it was eroding to where it was growing.

Signs and maps would explain that this was the shortest and best path to prevent erosion and point out that it could be used during all tides. And since the beach was growing, it had room for people to sit above high tide without damaging the dunes.

Fishermen preferred this area of the beach because they could wade out on a shallow sandbar and cast into deep holes where the striped bass waited for baitfish to be swept in on the incoming and outgoing tides.

The city could also consider moving the lifeguard's chair to this area and provide permanent Hibachi stoves so people wouldn't be tempted to build fires on the beach.

The Middle Path

The middle path would use the trail created when trucks drove through the dunes to repair the jetty in 2012. This path would only provide access to the beach at the low and middle tides but it was important to keep it open so official vehicles would have access to the middle of the beach in the event of an emergency.

City officials might not want to put a mobi-mat on this path to indicate that it was not a preferred path. But they might want to put a mobi-mat along the top of the dune for safety during the summer.

The South Path

This path would start at 69th street and take people out to the jetty where they could continue to the ocean or double back to the riverside beach. It would be used primarily by residents and people who rent houses on Northern Reservation Terrace. But people could also park at the public parking lot and walk down Northern Reservation Terrace to access this path during storms or extreme high tides. It could be indicated as the longer but safer path during such events.

In the end, the meeting revealed the paradox that almost losing the beach had also led to its resurrection. But the site visit to the area after the meeting revealed something else. We had lost significantly less of the beach this year than last year. Did the fact that the jetty had settled have something to do with it? I would have to investigate further.

CHAPTER 28
Grain by Grain
Plum Island Beach
March 2, 2017

Paul Crofts surveys the south jetty.

By early March, my hunch that something interesting was happening on Plum Island Beach was growing. At this time last year the beach had eroded by over a hundred feet in front of Northern Reservation Terrace. This year it had only eroded back forty feet.

The weather had certainly played a part. It had been an unusually calm winter with only a few storms in late January and early February. And of course the state's artificial dunes had done their sacrificial job. But it still seemed strange there had been more than twice as much erosion every year for the last three years than what we had seen during this year.

Could we already be seeing the effects of the jetty settling? Sandy Tilton said she had been wondering the same thing. Her photos showed that the north end of the beach had grown over a hundred feet since September. We wondered how much more the jetty would have to settle for the entire beach to start growing.

But I knew we needed something more than photographs to convince people that the jetty was settling that fast. So on another windy cold day in March we found ourselves back out on the beach showing the jetty to Paul Crofts. Paul taught surveying at Essex Technical High School and he and his colleague Ann Witzig, were interested in both profiling the beach and measuring how fast the jetty was settling. But the biggest problem was coming up with something stable enough to measure against. Everything on the beach was constantly moving and different parts of the jetty were settling at different rates.

But Paul thought he could build a platform on one of the jetty's boulders and measure its elevation against a water tower in Salisbury. His students could do this every month during the school year and Sandy and I could do it during the summer.

Our conversation with Paul spurred me to take another look at the Army Corps of Engineers' elevation drawings. The Corps had given them to us when we first noticed that the jetty was settling, almost three years before. But their print was small and I wasn't very proficient at reading elevations anyway, so I had just noticed the gross features and left it at that.

But a few days after our site visit I finally had time to sit down and look at the elevations carefully. I discovered that not only did they show the repairs, but they also had a line underneath the repairs that showed the height of the jetty before the repairs. It was a squiggly line that showed the exact height of each boulder. Not only that, it showed that the distance between the pre-repair and the post-repair jetty was only about two or three feet.

We had been assuming that the jetty might have to settle as much as four or five feet to get back to where it had been before the repairs. But this showed that now it only had to settle another foot or two to return to its pre-repair height.

It also meant that we were much further along in the process than we had formerly realized. We knew that the jetty was settling at the rate of about a foot a year so it would only take one to three years for the beach to start growing rather than the four or five we had been assuming it would take.

To put it another way, the jetty had already settled two feet, and that had been enough to allow 6,000 cubic yards of sand flow through the jetty to rebuild the beach. So nature was already providing more sand to the beach than the state had used to build the artificial dunes. It would only take another year or two for enough sand to start flowing through the jetty so that the beach could start growing again.

This might not seem very significant to people who live on the mainland, but to the 250 homeowners who lived on Northern Reservation Terrace it could mean the difference between losing their house in two years, or being safe for another twenty years.

CHAPTER 29
"Stella"
March 14, 2017

"Stella" Sandy Tilton photo.

It turns out that it is much easier to get into Mar-a-Lago without credentials than onto Plum Island without a resident ID.

I discovered this in the wake of winter storm Stella that blasted the island with driving snow and hurricane force winds on March 14. The winds left the telephone poles that lined Plum Island Turnpike at a 45-degree angle, and over a hundred Plum Island residents without electricity. This number climbed to over 400 people when National Grid sent repair trucks from as far away as Alabama to start turning off the power and replacing the old poles.

Newburyport police officers set up roadblocks to stop people from entering or leaving the island, then restricted the area to just people with resident ID's. They also helped drive people with infants or disabled family members to the Salvation Army's shelter where they could get warmth, medications and oxygen.

Some of the residents of Northern Reservation Terrace simply opted for the shelter rather than spending another cold dark night on the island. They remembered what it had been like two winters before when their basements filled with raw sewerage after the island's famously finicky sewerage system failed.

On March 17, I went out at low tide so I could walk on the beach. Unlike a traditional Northeaster that stalls off the coast for several days, Stella had blasted through in less than 12 hours so she had only been around for a single tidal cycle. So, like during a hurricane, the island had experienced more wind damage than erosion.

Newbury's seawall had failed in several places and the foundation of one of her out buildings had cracked. The main houses were all intact but slightly closer to the edge than you would want to be on a cold dark night with your house shuddering with the impact of each wave.

But the Merrimack River's South Jetty was a different story. It seemed like Stella had thrown all her forces at this single redoubt. Fourteen-foot waves had battered the jetty from both sides, washing sand through the structure from the oceanside and exploding up through the jetty from the riverside.

The waves had battered down the ten-foot high ridge of sand that guarded the jetty from ocean waves. This had allowed them to wash unimpeded through a stretch of the jetty that was as long as a football field.

This pounding had allowed about eight thousand cubic yards of sand to flow through the jetty to the riverside. Now that finely sifted sand lay in a pristine white sandbar over an acre in size and more than four feet deep. This was about two thousand more cubic yards of sand than had washed through the jetty during any storm the year before.

When I returned home and compared my photos of the jetty taken last year with those taken this year, I thought I could see why. It looked like Stella's relentless battering had made the jetty settle a few more inches.

It turned out that Stella had been the perfect storm for Plum Island Beach. It had not caused serious erosion like the waves from storms far out to sea that we had experienced last autumn. But its relentless pounding from short period waves had been enough to cause the jetty to settle. I couldn't wait for Paul Crofts Essex Tech students to get to the beach and measure exactly how much it had settled.

The Newbury and Newburyport communities' approach to erosion control were put in stark contrast by the storm. Residents of Newburyport were already working with the city, state and federal governments to rebuild the $150,000 sacrificial dunes that had saved them from winter storm Stella.

But the residents of Newbury had taken the law into their own hands, threatening to sue the town, state and federal government while rebuilding their multi-million dollar illegal seawall that had failed every year since 2013. And town and state officials fearing lawsuits had simply turned a blind eye to the transgressions.

The residents had also expected officials to spend over $25 Million to build anti-erosion devices and now they wanted them to spend hundreds of thousands of dollars to dredge sand from the Piscataqua River in Maine and pump it in front of their houses.

But people were starting to question why the public should pay for such big government projects that were so expensive, short-lived and only protected private property. Pumping sand from under George Charos's dock and using it to build two artificial dunes had been less expensive and far easier to get permitted.

Such a project would also require yearly maintenance. They reminded me of the mayor of a Columbian City who discovered that the best way to improve a neighborhood was to plant flowers. The first time he did it people stole them so he planted them again. This time neighbors started to landscape and protect the flower beds. After several more times the neighborhood developed a fierce pride in their plants and "Big Mommas" would shame any hoodlum who tried to harm their neighborhood flowers.

Through building fences and designing paths the residents had also gained a sense of ownership over "their beach." They were also learning how much people who had fished on this beach for years also loved and wanted to protect it. So they were developing a consensus that it would be worth the time and effort to keep rebuilding the sacrificial dunes until nature could rebuild the beach, like she did after the blizzard of 1978.

CHAPTER 30
Sand, Sand, Whose Got The Sand?
March 24, 2017

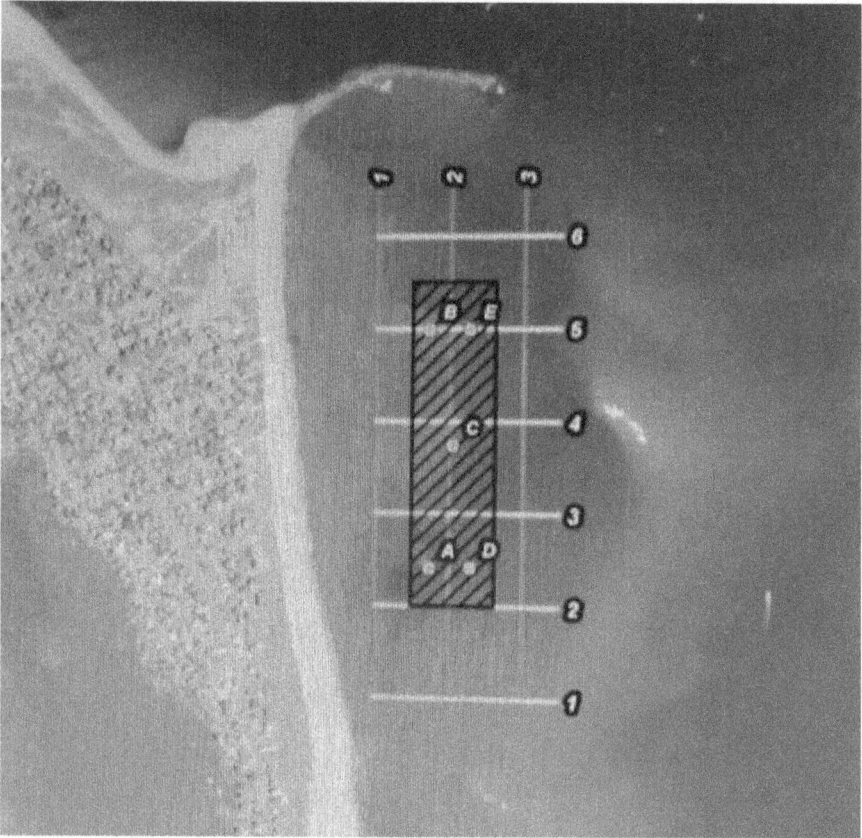

Proposed site for Piscataqua sand, south of South Jetty, USACE

On March 24, the Merrimack Beach Alliance met to discuss three potential sources of sand to renourish Plum Island. I decided to write about them from what I considered to be the least favorable to the most favorable renourishment solutions for the island.

First lets get rid of the most extreme of the "bigger is better" solutions. To be anywhere near successful at slowing down erosion on the entire length of the island, you would have to dump a million cubic yards of sand near the center of the island. This is never going to happen because there is no available source of that much sand. Plus it would be prohibitively expensive and the sand would have to be replaced every five to ten years anyway.

The next least favorable solution would be to use sand dredged from the Piscataqua River in Maine. This would provide 200,000 cubic yards of material but it would cost Massachusetts local and state agencies up to $2 million to transport the material and it would have to be dumped offshore because it consists of glacial till, not pure sand.

The next solution would use sand that the Army Corps of Engineers would dredge from the mouth of the Merrimack River in the next one to two years. But studies would have to be done and permits obtained to be able to pump this sand directly onto the beach at far greater expense.

But the sand could be offloaded into the nearshore disposal site, which has already been designated for the Piscataqua project. This site is just upstream of the South Jetty, so waves would slowly push it through the jetty and wash it down to the beach in front of Northern Reservation Terrace. It could be repeated whenever the river had to be dredged, which was be quite often.

But, the most favorable solution has already proved to be successful; rebuild the sacrificial dune system. This only cost the state $150,000 to make, partially from donated sand dredged from beneath the Captain's Lady's dock at the growing north end of the island.

It is still a little hard for the "bigger is better" guys to get their heads around the fact that this project which initially used an off the shelf dredge the size of a lawn mower and fourth graders to plant dune grass worked so well. I have to admit I was one of those skeptical at first

But the secret to why the project worked, and will work again, is redundancy. The dunes will have to be rebuilt and replanted for at least another year. But even if they have to be rebuilt for two more years it will be far less expensive and more successful than the other solutions.

Toward the end of the meeting, Vern Ellis, who so ably represents the residents of Northern Reservation Terrace, raised the issue that was on everyone's mind. George Charos was going to dredge below the Captain's Lady docks again in the spring. Wouldn't it make more sense and be far cheaper to put the sand directly on the sacrificial dunes rather than to truck the sand to Olga Way then truck it back again to rebuild the dunes in the Fall?

But this commonsense solution couldn't go forward because you can't have heavy equipment on the beach after April 1 when piping plovers arrive and start nesting. But nobody could remember plovers ever nesting on this portion of the beach because it had too much vegetation and too many steep scarps for the plovers to contend with. Plover adults like to be able to run up and down an unencumbered beach in order to feed their chicks.

When the Corps of Engineers drove through these same dunes to repair the jetty in 2014, they were required to hire a plover warden. It must have been about the biggest sinecure on the East Coast. I imagine he or she never saw a single plover all summer.

Such regulations were promulgated years before when it was decided to concentrate on protecting endangered species rather than whole habitats like barrier beaches. To me, concentrating on saving habitats makes more sense.

But if the state's Natural Heritage office could be persuaded that a plover warden would suffice, the dunes could be rebuilt and replanted in the spring. Then the dune grass would have all summer and all fall to create a matrix of roots as it grew up through the new dunes.

A state official pointed out that if the dune grass was planted in the spring it might be killed by hot weather. But the argument could also be made that most of the grass that students planted the spring before had survived. And even if some plants died in the summer they could be replaced with more plugs of grass in the fall.

At any rate, it seemed to be preferable to repeat this small successful project before next winter, rather than wait for one of the larger projects to materialize, or not, in the present environment of uncertain budgets and rapidly changing restrictions.

CHAPTER 31
ROB YOUNG

CHAPTER 31
Rob Young
March 29, 2017

Rob Young.

After Hurricane Matthew passed through in October, everyone gave a sigh of relief. It hadn't killed as many U.S. citizens as either Hurricane Sandy or Katrina. And it also hadn't damaged as many roads and homes as had been expected.

But coastal geologist Rob Young was less sanguine. The storm had torn up beaches and obliterated protecting sand dunes from Florida to Virginia including in Folly Beach, South Carolina.

Rob was the director of the Developed Shorelines Program at the University of Western Carolina, and the program had been using Folly Beach to study beach management for almost three decades. He knew the town's history of beach renourishment would have particular resonance for the residents of Plum Island.

In the 1890's Folly Beach's neighbor, Charleston, like Newburyport, had constructed jetties to stabilize the mouth of their harbor. But their jetties had also cut off the flow of sand to Folly Beach causing as much as 5 feet of erosion per year. The residents of Folly Beach then built seawalls to protect their homes, but the seawalls had destroyed the beach. So in 1994, the town convinced the Army Corps of Engineers to use dredged sand to both build up the beach and construct a berm to protect private property.

Two years later, both the berm and beach were gone, although the Corps had predicted they wouldn't have to be replaced for a decade. In fact the Corps argued that the beach was actually still there, but it was just underwater. To which the former director of the program, the irrepressible Orrin Pilkie replied, "True, but underwater sand is a very uncomfortable place to play volleyball." He was also known for likening the Army Corps of Engineers to a large water-loving dinosaur with fewer brains per pound of flesh than any other vertebrate.

So, Rob knew from experience that people would clamor for the federal government to pay to replace beaches after Hurricane Matthew, because The Federal Emergency Management Agency had decided that if dunes and beaches had been put in place to protect coastal property they should be considered infrastructure. That meant that even if a community hadn't suffered any property damage it could still be eligible to receive millions of federal dollars to repair its beaches.

Did FEMA's determination mean that the two artificial dunes that Massachusetts had built to protect the houses on Northern Reservation Terrace would also come with their own implicit guarantee? If storms washed the dunes away during a declared emergency, would FEMA be on the hook to replace them? Or should the United States adopt an entirely different approach to our coasts in the new era of sea level rise? People would find out when Rob gave his Storm Surge lecture at the Newburyport City Hall and at an informal dinner beforehand.

CHAPTER 32
Legalities
April 2017

Sand scraping.

In April, Plum Island would revert to a totally unfair situation. While Newburyport and every other community in the Commonwealth would be spending time and paying hundreds of thousand of dollars in fees to get permission to build legal anti-erosion structures, residents in Newbury would be paying nothing to repair their illegal seawalls, all while town and state officials looked the other way.

The seawalls had made their neighbors homes more vulnerable to erosion and had ruined the public beach. The residents had also hired an expensive lobbyist to circumvent the Army Corps of Engineers' regulations so they could repair the South Jetty, which had put 250 homes at risk in Newburyport's Northern Reservation Terrace neighborhood.

So, how had they gotten away with this? When the town and state turned down their request to build a seawall the residents had gone to the Pacific Legal Foundation, the most powerful anti-environmental organization in the country and had them call then Governor Deval Patrick's office and threaten to sue. The state backed down half an hour later.

When Storm Surge's speaker Rob Young heard this story his response was, "Why doesn't someone sue the neighbors, the Corps or even the state for not enforcing its own regulations? The Pacific Legal Foundation sues people all the time and most of the time they lose."

His response initiated a long discussion about the pros and cons of suing. The state's legal department had backed down because they felt the Commonwealth might lose, even though other states including the Carolinas, Florida and Texas had all made seawalls illegal. They only allowed communities to renourish their beaches with sand that was becoming increasingly difficult to find.

The residents of Northern Reservation Terrace, the City of Newburyport or the state, which had just paid $150,000 to build the artificial dunes, could all have standing to sue.

But would it be wise? The Pacific Legal Foundation would like nothing better than to sue the most liberal state in the nation and they might even have a chance of winning under the takings clause of the Constitution's 5th amendment.

It would resurrect old wounds and pit the neighboring communities of Newbury and Newburyport against each other. Plus the state might not want to ban seawalls outright when its present regulations restrict them in most cases anyway.

So in many ways our present regulatory situation is like the jetty before it was repaired. Both systems work, but both systems leak. And as unfair and unsatisfactory as that might sound, it might be the best solution we can come up with, keep the leaky regulatory system and let nature return the jetty to its former leaky self.

The leaky jetty will let sand sneak through to rebuild Plum Island Beach and the leaky regulatory system will let scofflaws squeeze through the cracks. They will be able to get away with breaking these human laws and might even prevail against the Constitution for a few years. But they wont be able to break Mother Nature's laws for more than a decade. She always bats last and she always wins.

CHAPTER 33
Theseus
A Not Very Funny April Fool's Storm
April 2, 2017

Another acre of sand four feet deep was pushed through the jetty by winter storm Theseus.

Vern Ellis got up early on April 2. He wanted to see what winter storm Theseus had done to the dunes in front of his Northern Reservation Terrace home.

Theseus had been the exact opposite of winter storm Stella. It sat 800 miles offshore, building waves that had become ten-foot high monsters by the time they reached Plum Island. They then pounded the island as the storm dropped first snow, then sleet, then rain.

Nobody had appreciated the lousy April Fool's joke that caused more erosion but less wind damage than Stella.

Vern saw that the storm had torn another 5 to 10 feet off the dunes but he also saw where waves had washed more sand through the jetty. Now three acre sized sandbars hugged the riverside of the structure.

The most recent sandbar from Theseus lay stretched out along the seaward end of the jetty. The sandbar from Stella lay clumped up in the middle of the jetty while the sandbar left from the February storms had already snaked around the spur of the jetty and was starting to protect the houses on Northern Reservation Terrace. The sandbars weren't enough to solve the problem but they were a decent first step until the Corps could act.

But it was what Vern saw that evening at high tide that had concerned him the most. Scores of people were walking on the leading edge of the dune, where the winter storms had deposited almost a foot of new sand.

Spring was normally when the dune grass would start growing up through the new sand leaving a matrix of roots to bind together the dune below. This is how the front of the dune grows to become the primary dune, nature's first bulwark against coastal erosion.

However dune grass dies when people walk on it or make a path through it because sand will slough off the grass onto the path, which kills the grass after their roots are exposed for only a few days.

When the state's Department of Conservation and Recreation prepared the beach for the summer, it had been limited by two conditions. Another agency, the state's Natural Heritage office stipulated that the work had to be completed by April 1st when plover were supposed to start nesting. Plus they stipulated that the DCR had to use ropes tied to poles instead of snow fencing that had worked so effectively at keeping people off the dunes the summer before.

This year they would have to use this symbolic fencing so plover could make their way to the beach. The problem was, nobody had ever seen a piping plover on this part of the beach because it had too much vegetation and its scarps were too steep for the birds to clamber down them. The birds liked broad new overwash areas where they could run up and down the beach unencumbered by vegetation and drop-offs.

The other problem was that the symbolic fencing looked just like a ropewalk so people were using it as a handrail as they trampled a path through the most fragile and important keystone species of the dune itself. So you had one state agency fixated on protecting a single species, that wasn't there, against another state agency trying to protect the habitat that the entire ecosystem depended on.

It was a conundrum that only Bruce Tarr could solve and he would get his chance at the next meeting of the Merrimack River Beach Alliance in April.

CHAPTER 34
A Totally Unfortunate Discovery
April 2, 2017

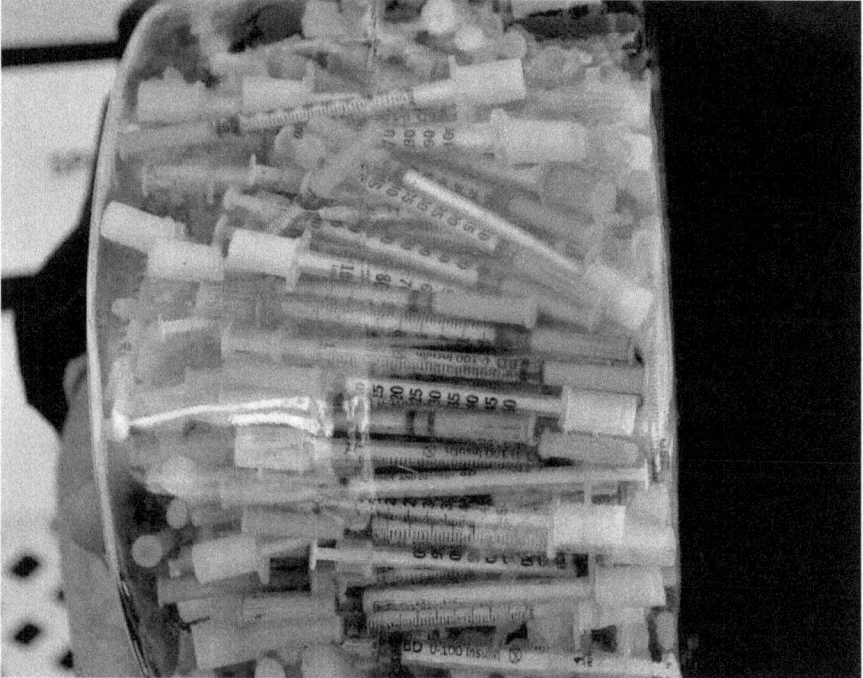

Rocky Morrison displays a fishbowl of syringes collected from the Merrimack River.

After taking photographs of the aftermath of winter storm Theseus I decided to lie on the beach to soak up the early April sun. A pair of surfers were riding the brilliant white breakers and a few families were enjoying the beach.

Suddenly a Newbury police officer entered the beach near the refuge and started to walk toward a couple walking their two dogs. It was the day after the plover were supposed to arrive, so I figured I was about to witness a dog-poop bust.

But the officer seemed to be more intent on looking for something in the sand. Finally he pulled out some latex gloves and picked a syringe out of the wrackline. I didn't have the presence of mind to take a picture and thought it was probably just an isolated incident anyway, so I continued to sit back and enjoy the sun.

But when I got home I saw that Walt Thompson had posted a picture of a needle he had taken just north of Newbury's Center groin. Someone else mentioned that the year before, he had seen the Newbury Fire Marshall with a whole bag of syringes he had collected from Plum Island. And I remembered that when I first moved to Ipswich in 2001 I found needles along the shore that I naively assumed had been from someone with diabetes.

Then on April 3rd I saw an indignant story on New Hampshire television about a Massachusetts group that wanted to string a boom across the Merrimack to prove that thousands of needles were flowing down the river from New Hampshire.

Everyone on our public forum tried to explain these observations based on past experiences. Most of us remembered the summer of 1987, when medical wastes washed up on the Jersey Shore after a company from New York had illegally dumped them off a municipal pier.

So our first assumption was that the needles probably came from people who used them for medical purposes. But this didn't quite ring true. If a doctor prescribes you syringes for a medical condition he usually also gives you a plastic container to store the used needles in so you can return them to the hospital for disposal.

Companies have lucrative contracts for the safe disposal of such needles. Why would they risk jeopardizing their business by doing something foolhardy like dumping just needles, but no other medical wastes, into the Merrimack River?

The other former incident that everyone remembered was when the wastewater treatment plant in Hookset New Hampshire had accidentally released hundreds of thousands of wafer thin filter discs into the Merrimack. They continue to appear from Maine to Cape Cod after every storm and high course tide.

So perhaps the needles came through upstream sewer systems. But why would someone with a medical condition throw their used needles down the toilet when it would be so much easier to keep them in their plastic container?

That left the ugly alternative that perhaps heroin users had flushed the needles down toilets after injection. I'm sorry, but I don't care how stoned you are, you don't want to be strung out and have your toilet backed up as well.

Nope, the unfortunate conclusion seemed to be that thousands of needles had been left on streets or in out-of-the-way places where people had bought and used drugs. Then storms had washed the needles into the river where they had floated like a cork from places like New Hampshire, Lowell, Lawrence, Haverhill, Amesbury, Newburyport and Newbury down onto the beaches of Plum Island and beyond. It was an unsettling indicator of exactly how widespread and close to home our opioid epidemic had become.

CHAPTER 35
The Encampment
April 8, 2017

The encampment.

The discovery of needles on Plum Island had set off a chain of events that led me to Methuen, Massachusetts where I met Rocky Morrison at the offices of the Clean River Project. It sat amidst auto repair shops, and was surrounded by rusty cars, motorcycles, anchors and even a pistol they had hauled out of the Merrimack River.

Five float boats were tied to the docks in back of the building. Rocky had built them by hand and used them to anchor booms along the river to catch floating debris. It was the floating debris that I was interested in, and inside his office Rocky had a supersized fish bowl that held over a thousand syringes he had collected in his booms. During the last few years he had collected dozens, this year they numbered in the hundreds if not thousands.

Rocky drove along Water Street to see where some of the needles had come from. It was a warm sunny day and we entered an attractive riverside park. The river was surging over the Lawrence Dam and the water was rising fast.

We made our way along a rocky cliff and under the Lawrence Bridge where a homeless man had built a shelter out of wooden palettes. It was a dramatic site tucked safely against the buttress of the bridge and sat right beside the water plunging over the 35-foot high stone dam.

But an open sleeping bag and old cloths were floating ominously in the rising waters and the occupant was nowhere to be found. His belongings were strewn along the riverbank and we saw used syringes every four or five feet. Several were inches from being swept into the rising river; others were already floating in the shallows.

Further down the river we came to five more tents and under the next bridge there were 4 more encampments that held half a dozen tents each. Tables were set up and a guy came by offering orange juice out of a jug. Piss bottles seemed to be everywhere amidst the clutter of old clothes and collapsed furniture. The inhabitants used the bottles to avoid the smell of urine in the rat-infested encampment.

Three young men in long gray cowls and sandals walked slowly through the encampment. These were from a new order of Trappist monks who had taken vows to administer to the homeless and live themselves in outdoor shelters. It was hard to say if they looked more like Obi-Wan Kenobi, or something out of a dystopic movie, but they gave the encampment a creepy medieval feel.

Most of the tents were new and shut tight. Their occupants were out panhandling to satisfy their $150 a day habit. It was not an easy life.

Probably 25 to 30 people lived in the encampment. Most had stashes of clean needles they had reportedly been able to pick up free at CVS in exchange for used needles. Most of the inhabitants had to inject themselves three or four times a day to keep heroin's debilitating lows in check, so just this short section of the river might account for 75 to 120 needles a day.

Most of the needles were strewn haphazardly through the encampment but almost all of them were resheathed so nobody would get stuck and infected. But all it would take would be a single rainstorm to wash a big pulse of needles off the adjacent streets and into the nearby river. It was a sobering to think of kids finding the needles, sheathed or not, on Plum Island or in places like Newbury-port's beautiful Maudsley Park.

Shortly after this chapter appeared in the Newburyport Daily News, the New-buryport City Council voted to give the Clean Water Project in Methuen $8,000 to use booms to clean up needles and other floating debris from the Merrimack River. Other communities were expected to do the same.

CHAPTER 36
A River Runs Through it ... Again
April 13, 2017

A River runs through it ....again! Ipswich River on April 12, 2017.

On April 13, Wayne Castonguay, Geoffrey Day and I traced the 35-mile course of the Ipswich River. Wayne leads the Ipswich River Watershed Association and Geoff is head of a coalition of groups trying to bring sea run brook trout back to New England rivers and streams.

Our plan was to repeat the same trip we had made last August when the river had gone bone dry; killing off fish, turtles, frogs, lizards, salamanders, insects and the plankton that supported the entire ecosystem. That was to say nothing of the water supply of the 14 towns and cities that normally removed 32 million gallons of water from the river's watershed every day. In essence the river had died and we wanted to see its resurrection.

Our first stop was the Willowdale dam above the Foote Brothers kayak and canoe rental emporium. This was where the United States Geological Survey has a gauge that measures the river's flow. Last year less than a cubic foot of water was passing through the weir every second. Today 600 cubic feet of water were flowing through the weir and only five days ago over 1200 cubic feet were surging through every second.

It seemed like a good sign. The El Niño system that had started the drought two years ago was back to neutral and wasn't expected to kick in again until autumn. Massachusetts officials would soon be able to declare that the drought was over and people could start watering their lawns again.

But Wayne was not so sanguine. He pointed to where the height of the flood was only five days before. The river had already dropped several feet in less than a week. It was this yoyo pattern of rapid flooding and receding that worried Castonquay the most.

The problem was not just how much rain fell during the year, but what was happening to all that rain. Back in the 17th century, when this river was supplying water for people, fish and agriculture as well as powering scores of grain mills, saw mills, textile mills and distilleries, rain soaked into the soft soil of fields and forests to be stored in the groundwater of the river's watershed.

Now rain was rushing off of hard, impermeable surfaces like streets and parking lots, then flowing directly into the river, causing this pattern of floods and droughts. Under natural conditions a river like the Ipswich River would be able to withstand a few droughty years, but now so little water was getting into the groundwater that the river would die during a droughty year like 2016 and it would take at least a decade for it to fully recover, if no more droughts occurred, an exceedingly unlikely event.

Like the erosion on Plum Island caused by human structures, the death of this river was not a natural disaster, but a man-made tragedy.

But there were signs of hope. Upstream of us, two of Wayne's employees were "tuning" a fish ladder so herring could get around the dam. They were doing this by adjusting the ladder's baffles so the flow of water would slow down enough for the herring to be able swim against the current and up over the dam into the pond. But when they removed the baffles, the young men found the baffles were covered with hundreds of the wriggling insect larvae. Nature's inherent resilience was fighting back.

Our next stop was the Wenham pump station. It had just finished pumping water out of the river and into Wenham Lake, where it would be stored for water use during the summer. Thirteen other communities did the same thing.

In fact Ninety percent of the river's water was pumped out of wells in the river's watershed or out of the river itself. The water was then used for drinking, watering lawns, washing cars and wastewater. Much of the wastewater ended up in the Massachusetts Water Resources Authority system, which was then pumped into Boston harbor. So only ten percent of the Ipswich River's water ever made it to the Atlantic Ocean through the river's mouth. Imagine how confusing that would be for a sea run brook trout looking for its natal stream!

But by the end of the day, we realized that like the erosion season on Plum Island, the drought would soon be over. But would it be just another Pyrrhic victory?

CHAPTER 37
Sand Sculpting
April 23, 2017

Sand sculptor G Augustine Lynas. Courtesy NWPT Film Festival.

On April 21, the Newburyport Daily News ran a photo of the sand sculptor G. Augustine Lynas carefully shaping a large, perfectly rounded sand dome that would have made Brunelleschi proud. The accompanying article invited people to drop by to see Lynas build one of his futuresque sand castles on Plum Island.

The announcement took everyone on the MRBA by surprise. Nobody knew whether half a dozen, a dozen or several dozen people would make the long trek down the beach to see the sculpting project. What disturbed them the most was that the event had been scheduled for high tide, when people would be forced to walk through the dunes.

Residents had already seen children rolling down the face of the 20-foot high scarp, threatening to maim both the dunes and themselves on broken glass and pieces of rusty metal that jutted from the remains of the old coast guard station.

It was a stark reminder of just how ill prepared officials were for the rapidly approaching summer season. By this time last year Gregg Moore from the University of New Hampshire had already arranged for students to replant the dunes and for residents to put up miles of snow fencing.

The snow fencing had worked remarkably well not only at trapping sand, but at keeping people from trampling through the newly sprouted dune grass. This year however, the Department of Conservation and Recreation was being thwarted by the state's own Natural Heritage Program.

The heritage officials had determined that the DCR had to use ropes and posts so that piping plover could run under the ropes, as we have seen.

The officials had even declined Senator Tarr's invitation to attend the MRBA meeting. They had probably confused the MRBA with the MBBA, the Massachusetts Beach Buggy Association. State officials knew to take several doses of anti-anxiety medication in order to get through the MBBA meetings with a modicum of equanimity. So Senator Tarr decided to invite the natural Heritage folks once again and stress that the MRBA was a problem-solving group not a platform for adversarial rhetoric.

On April 23 I went to see how many people would show up for the sand sculpturing. But the event had been canceled, "due to weather and unfavorable sand conditions".

Hmm, it was a bright sunny day and the sand looked just fine, but it was probably just as well. There were already too many people walking through the dunes when I arrived at 10 am for the morning's high tide.

The other issue that the MRBA members had discussed was Senator Tarr's announcement that the state's legislative committee had finally voted for the $2 million environmental bond to pay for either the Piscatagua, or the Merrimack sand disposal projects.

The Piscataqua project would pump about 350,000 cubic yards of sand just off Plum Island and the Merrimack project might pump less than half that amount directly onto the beach in front of the houses on Northern Reservation Terrace.

So it came down to the difference between putting a smaller amount of sand directly where you wanted it to be, or putting a larger amount of sand just offshore and letting nature decide where she wanted it to be.

It sounded counter intuitive, but if the Woods Hole Group research was accurate, putting a larger amount of sand offshore could be the best solution. But in the end the decision would probably come down to which project would be cheaper and easier to permit.

Meanwhile, almost nothing had been said about the project to use the sand dredged from under George Charos's dock to rebuild the artificial dunes. Hopefully that smaller project would get permitted and quietly proceed while officials debated whether to pursue the two larger projects that would not happen until 2019 — at the very earliest.

CHAPTER 38
My Non-Science Science March
April 22, 2017

Plum Island "Science March".

On April 22nd, I didn't go to any of the marches for science. Over 500 hundred of them were being held around the world, with the largest in Washington D.C., but the one in my old hometown, Woods Hole, had the highest percentage of it population in attendance. That was pretty easy, 90% of its residents are scientists anyway, so if they just all walked to the Post at the same time they would have a larger science march than most cities.

One of the goals of the march was to have people see that some of their neighbors were scientists. But my family had experienced culture shock in the other direction. When we lived in Woods Hole all of our friends were scientists, engineers or technicians, but when we moved to Charlestown everyone we met seemed to be a lawyer — or else needed one fast!

One of the largest marches was in Boston, so I certainly could have gone and probably would have gone twenty years before. But I had watched global warming morph from being perceived as a simple scientific problem to a political football by the great communicator Ronald Reagan. And I didn't doubt for a minute that Donald Trump had the ability to do the same for science itself.

Interestingly enough, I felt that science writers rather than scientists presented the most thoughtful arguments for attending a march or not. You had the feeling they had more experience with the perils of being misperceived by the public than scientists who mostly speak to other scientists.

One science writer stated that he never gave money to political causes in order to stay above the fray. Other writers pointed out that their employers prohibited them from participating in such events. Perhaps the most insightful comment came from a woman who said she was an observer by nature and if she attended a march it would be with her notebook and pencil in hand.

My reason for not attending was far more mundane. I felt that I spent every other day of the week writing about global warming and sea level rise, usually without mentioning either phenomenon by name.

I tried to just tell the story of what it is like to live on a coast that is changing so dramatically, rather than hitting people over the head with facts and figures about climate change. I think I might have even changed the minds of a few people who are dealing with these issues everyday.

So why would I want to alienate anyone by attending a march where you can only say what you can fit on a 2' by 3' placard? Isn't that akin to firing off a tweet, like other people we know?

CHAPTER 39
The Survey
April 28, 2017

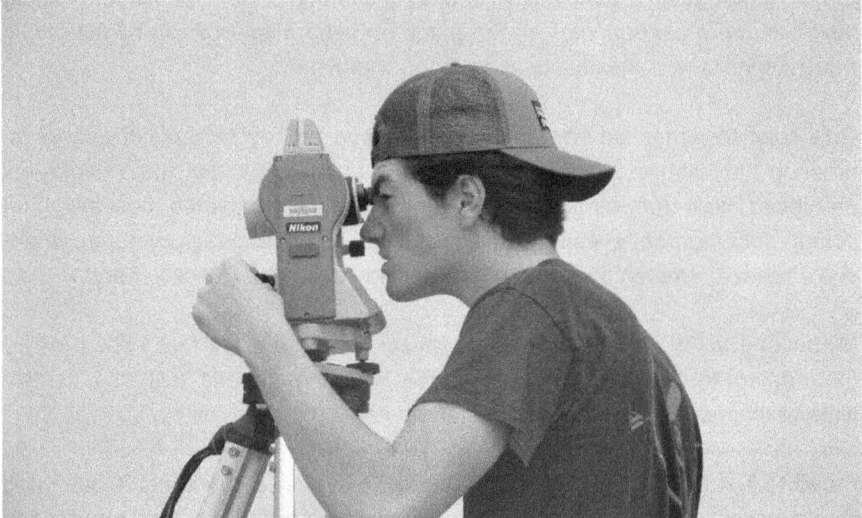

Toby Johnson surveys the South Jetty.

On April 28, Plum Island was engulfed in a cold gray shawl of fog. I couldn't see Salisbury. I couldn't see the ocean. I couldn't see any sign of another human being. This was a problem because I was supposed to meet Paul Croft's students from Essex Tech at 10am.

So I decided to walk out to the end of the jetty just to make sure. Halfway there I spotted the students intently inspecting the wrackline. What had they found? I took a few more steps and watched the students magically morph into a flock of fog-enshrouded seagulls. These conditions sure weren't going to make it easy to survey the jetty.

But a moment later the fog lifted just enough so I could see a spot of sunlight on the far shore. Then it got uncomfortably warm. I was still wearing an anorak I had worn to fight the morning chill, now it was just oppressive.

I figured the fog was so thick that Paul had canceled the field trip so I decided to return to my car and get rid of my coat. I also knew there was a big juicy chicken salad sandwich I had been saving for just such an emergency.

But as I walked back through the dunes I started to hear disembodied voices floating up from the beach. So I yelled through the fog.

"Are you from Essex Tech?"

"Yes."

"Great! I'll meet you at the end of the jetty in a few minutes."

That gave me just enough time to ditch my coat, take a swig of water and gobble down my sandwich before looking for the students in the fog. When I found them, a marine biologist was giving them an impromptu talk about marine debris, so I had a chance to catch up with Paul.

He had already briefed the students and separated them into three groups. Each group had to evaluate the situation and figure out the best way to survey the jetty.

It was a difficult problem. You had to assume that everything on the beach was unstable and that some parts of the jetty were settling faster than others.

I joined a group that wanted to set up their survey equipment on several of the larger boulders and sight from them to a stationary navigation beacon. Then they planned to flash a laser at the beacon on the other side of the river. The problem with this solution was that the students had to make sure the survey equipment could be set up at exactly the same height on its tripod legs when they repeated the measurements every month.

The idea was to get one solid measurement to use as baseline data in June, and then take another measurement when school started again in the fall. Then, if all went well, they would retake measurements every month during the winter's erosion season.

The second team had decided to place the survey equipment directly on the boulders to avoid the difficulty of setting up the tripod legs at exactly the same height for each measurement.

The third team had come up with the idea of measuring from the boulders that were settling fastest, back to the boulders that appeared to be more stable. Even though the entire jetty was settling, this method would measure the dip where the jetty was settling faster. It could also be done in a thick fog!

By the end of the day each team would have enough data so they could debrief the other teams and decide which method they would use when they returned to make their real measurements in June.

It had been an instructive day and I knew the rest of my sandwich was waiting for me back in the car. What I didn't know was whether to eat it after it had been sitting in the sun, which had finally deigned to come out. I decided to eat it anyway, and paid the price that night.

CHAPTER 40
The Meeting
May 4, 2017

Beach Access.

The renowned science writer Lewis Thomas once described the sound made by scientists at the end a lecture as, "the most extraordinary noise, half-shout, half-song made by simultaneously raised human voices explaining things to each other".

By that criterion the second meeting of the Plum Island Beach access committee was a great success. But it hadn't started out that way. Tensions were high. Someone had written a letter to the Newburyport Daily News saying that there wasn't enough scientific evidence to show that walking through the dunes was causing erosion to Plum Island Beach and that the problem was the jetty itself.

The letter was beside the point. In the short term, there wasn't anything you could do about the jetty but you could protect dunes, which were nature's first line of defense.

The first meeting of the beach access committee had been exquisitely choreographed with formal presentations and an exercise so that everyone could map out where they thought you should be able walk to the beach. But this second meeting had gotten off to a ragged start.

From the get-go there had been an anti-government sentiment in the room. People started going off in tangents and asking hostile questions, intimating that they thought the system was rigged and the government was just going to do what they wanted to do anyway.

This was strange since the state had provided a $25,000 grant specifically designed to elicit people's input. City Councilor Sharif Zeid finally offered to moderate the public comment part of the meeting. Standing well over six feet tall, nobody was going to question his authority.

One-by-one people vented their concerns. The main critic of the process repeated his contention that there had not been adequate usage data. Another person wanted to know why they hadn't received a survey from the Plum Island Surfcasters Association. Others were upset that they only had five options to choose from.

It seemed that ninety percent of the people who went to the beach used the public parking lot and three main paths to get to the water. Only one or two people argued for using a fourth path that ran through the artificial dune that the state had just built and almost a hundred middle school students had just planted. It didn't seem like the handful of critics actually used the beach that much. They just didn't want the government to tell them what to do and didn't want to have to walk a hundred extra steps to get to the beach. But, by the end of the meeting, everyone had been able to express their point of view.

Then, after the formal meeting broke up, people started congregating in small knots explaining their ideas to each other. A few people walked across the room to engage those whom they had disagreed with in public and that joyous descant that Lewis Thomas wrote about rose through the rafters of Pita Hall. It had been a good meeting after all.

CHAPTER 41
"Good Prank"
May 9, 2017

Quick driveby, Mar-a-Lago.

"Good Prank," laughed FBI director James Comey when the news flashed across the television screen that he had just been fired by Donald Trump. But, just to make sure, he ducked into an enjoining room of the bureau's downtown office in Los Angeles to check.

Sure enough Trump had done the unthinkable — once again. In the midst of being investigated by the FBI, the CIA, the NSA, plus subcommittees of the House and Senate, the President had fired Director Comey, expecting Republicans to back him and Democrats not to complain very loudly because of Comey's handling of Hillary Clinton's e-mails.

Such behavior had always worked for the real estate mogul before. If you make a mistake, simply fire someone else and hire a good lawyer. Only this wasn't a real estate company whose deal had just gone south.

This was the government of the United States with its checks, balances, and multiple sectors all keeping an eye on each other. To say nothing of the national press who Trump had demonized throughout the campaign, the inaugural and his first hundred days in office. Didn't he know the old saw, never pick a fight with someone who buys ink by the barrel?

So the nation had been transfixed as Comey's motorcade wound through L.A. traffic to the LAX airport where he had to board a private plane to fly back to Washington. Then they were appalled that evening as they watched Sean Spicer hiding behind trees on the White House lawn before scooting to a side door and locking himself in to avoid speaking to the press.

But eventually Sean Spicer did emerge and ordered cameramen to turn off their lights before trying to explain that firing Comey had all been because of a letter written by the justice department's newly appointed Deputy Director Rod Rosenstein. Of course Trump had his personal bodyguard deliver the official letter to the FBI headquarters when he knew the director would be out of town. It seemed our tone-deaf president couldn't even manage a decent cover-up.

I found it awfully difficult to write about paths on Plum Island beach when such momentous events were taking place in our Capital. But it was even worse than that.

I stood to lose 50 cents on a bet I had made with the head of the Newburyport Conservation Commission. I had bet Joe Teixeira that Rex Tillerson would convince Trump to have the United States stay in the Paris Climate Accords.

Now the White House wouldn't have time to deal with the issue that could help decide the fate of barrier beaches like Plum Island. I would lose my 50 cents after having so cleverly forced Joe to back Steve Bannon and the White House's forces of darkest evil.

But I was also forced to grapple with the question of what the hell was I doing writing about beach paths when our country was going through a constitutional crisis? I was able to take comfort from John Steinbeck words when he was writing about collecting marine invertebrates in the midst of World War II, "It either all seemed very important, or none of it seemed very important at all."

CHAPTER 42
Backcast Thinking
May 12, 2017

Waves in the Merrimack River.

At the May 12 meeting of the MRBA the Army Corps of Engineers detailed the status of seven studies it was conducting from Salisbury to Essex. Two features stood out with particular clarity.

First they described the potential sources of sand that could be used for beach renourishment. These included the 725,000 cubic yards of sand and glacial till they planned to dredge from the upper turning basin of Maine's Piscataqua River. They emphasized that as soon as the river was dredged they would deliver the material to whichever communities had completed their studies and had permits in hand to receive the material.

Bob Boeri from the Massachusetts Coastal Zone Management Office said that, "you are never going to find sand this inexpensive again," and stressed that several other communities like Hull could win the sand if North Shore communities didn't get their act together.

Other sources would include 35,000 cubic yards of sand dredged from the Essex River, which Essex was going to spread on its marshes to induce them to keep up with sea level rise, plus between 200,000 and 500,00 cubic yards of sand, which could be dredged from the ebb and flood tide deltas of the Merrimack River.

The ebb tide delta extended beyond the mouth of the Merrimack River and the flood tide delta pushed into the river. The sand that George Charos had already dredged from beneath his docks could be considered to be part of the flood tide delta and thus a precedent for further use of this sand to protect houses on Northern Reservation Terrace.

If you added up all the sources of sand you had about a million cubic yards of sand available to all the communities that applied for it. But it would take two to five years and a lot of work for Plum Island to get even a modest portion of that sand.

Then the Corps' Mark Habel dropped a bombshell. He explained that the Corps could study the possibility of using sand from the Merrimack River to stabilize the Northern Reservation Terrace area. On the face of it this seemed like the ideal solution. The state's artificial dune built with sand dredged from beneath George Charos's dock had already worked. But the proposed study also highlighted a huge Catch-22 in the Corp's regulations.

The Corps had to do a cost benefit analysis for all its projects. For instance, when Newbury applied for a similar project they could point to the economic loss of all their houses that had washed away. But the Corps could only look at losses that had already occurred, not at loses that will happen. In other words the Corps could only hindcast past losses not forecast future losses.

Northern Reservation Terrace provided the perfect example of the flaws of not being able to forecast. The beach had been eroding 150 feet a year since the jetty repairs had been finished in 2014. Now the houses on Northern Reservation Terrace had less than 80 feet between them and the ocean. At that rate they stood to lose as many as 20 houses in two years and up to 250 houses in the decades ahead.

But according to the Corps regulations, the 400 feet of beaches and dunes had no economic value and they couldn't use forecasts to determine eligibility. This sounded like hindcast thinking to some attendees and backcast thinking to others.

CHAPTER 43
The Gift
May 20, 2017

George Charos dredging operation.

Massachusetts, Newburyport, and the residents of Northern Reservation Terrace owed a huge debt of gratitude to George Charos for providing sand to build the dual dune system that had helped save their houses during the 2017 winter erosion season.

He had taken the initiative to buy his small dredge, and hire an engineer to obtain the necessary permits to dredge sand from beneath his docks. It was a long and arduous process that had to be repeated every season, though it would have seemed to make sense for the order of conditions to last for at least a full year.

It had been a large project for George's small family-run business whose busy charter fishing and whale-watching season ran from spring through the fall.

Since the city, state and residents had all benefited from the sand, it would seem to make sense that they could all chip in to help him repeat the dredging operation in the future.

The Corps of Engineers has estimated that between 100,000 and 250,000 cubic yards of sand could be dredged from the Merrimack River's flood tide delta. Part of that delta was making George's area unnavigable. This meant that the area around his docks could provide a large source of easily permitable local sand for as long as the Northern Reservation Terrace area needed it.

One obvious organization to take on this effort would be the Merrimack River Beach Alliance. The MRBA already included the state's Department of Conservation and Recreation that owns the beach where the sand would be used, the city of Newburyport that manages the beach and the residents of Northern Reservation Terrace who would be protected by the sand, plus the federal, state and town agencies responsible for issuing the necessary permits.

Such a project would provide a model for other areas that have similar sources of easily accessible sand to protect their coasts.

CHAPTER 44
Revisions
May 24, 2017

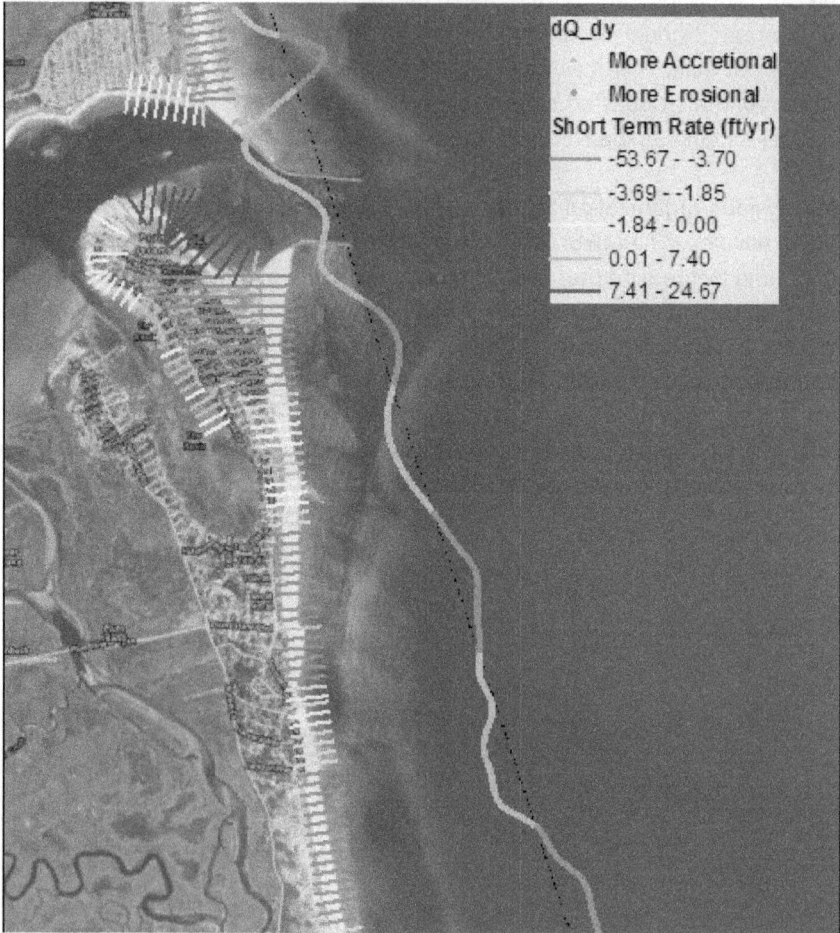

Graphic of Plum Island Point erosion and accretion, courtesy Woods Hole Group.

On May 24, Matt Shultz presented the Woods Hole Group's Plum Island sediment transport analysis to the general public. It was the same study they had presented to the MRBA in preliminary form in February.

But in February the results of the study had been crystal clear. Ninety percent of the time longshore currents carried sand from the center of Plum Island north and from the center of the island south.

But this iteration of the study showed the pitfalls of conducting science by committee. The study had been done by a loose consortium of institutions including the Army Corps of Engineers, Boston University and the Virginia Institute of Marine Sciences.

A local academic panel had also reviewed the study, though you would be hard pressed to find any of the members who held an actual held academic position. Apparently they had convinced the Woods Hole group to include the PhD thesis of a VIMS student to round out their consensus.

But the thesis was a throwback to the old idea that southward flowing currents were responsible for building an offshore sandbar that caused a hot spot of erosion in the groinfield in front of Annapolis Way. But the thesis had the causality backwards.

It was not the sandbar that was causing erosion near the groinfield, but the groinfield that had broken through the continuous sandbar that lies off most barrier beach islands. The hole in the sandbar allowed sand to flow into the deep water where it was lost to the sand transport system. Some people had advocated dumping glacial till from the Picataqua River into the hole but the hole in the sandbar would just be scoured out again as long as the groinfield remained in place.

But the Woods Hole Group's public presentation did provide some useful new information. Their model calculated that on average about 70,000 cubic yards of sand flowed from the center of the island south every year, and about 30,000 cubic yards of sand flowed from the center of the island north.

This meant that during Northeasters, sand could be washed south of the center of the island. Then after the storm passed, the longshore currents would carry the sand past Sandy Point where it would escape the Plum Island system. Of course it would enter the Crane's Beach sediment transport system, which would be too bad for Plum Island but fine for folks who lived in Ipswich.

But the 30,000 cubic yards of sand that flowed north would bode well for residents on the north end of the island. Since the jetty had been repaired in 2014 it had settled about two and a half feet. So the amount of sand flowing through the jetty had risen from essentially nothing in 2014, to between 16,000 and 24,000 cubic yards in 2017.

So the jetty only needed to settle about two more feet, before the 30,000 cubic yards of sand flowing through the jetty would match the 30,000 cubic yards of sand flowing from the center of the island north. When this happened, the beach in front of Northern Reservation Terrace would start growing again.

At the present rate that the jetty was settling it would only take one or two more years for this to happen. Then, the immediate crisis facing the residents of Northern Reservation Terrace would be over.

www.ingramcontent.com/pod-product-compliance
Lightning Source LLC
Chambersburg PA
CBHW032145020426
42334CB00016B/1234